The Complete
Shabbat Table
Companion

THE
JEWISH
LEARNING GROUP

THE COMPLETE
SHABBAT TABLE COMPANION
RABBI ZALMAN GOLDSTEIN

"10th ANNIVERSARY EDITION"

Copyright © 1996-2010

THE
JEWISH
LEARNING GROUP

Tel. 1-(888)-56-LEARN
www.JewishLearningGroup.com
Email: Info@JewishLearningGroup.com

ISBN-10: 1-891293-11-7
ISBN-13: 978-1-891293-11-5

Acknowledgements

A special thanks is due to Rabbi Nissan Mindel, Editor-in-Chief of Kehot Publications, for permitting the inclusion of excerpts and ideas from his outstanding (and popular) book *"My Prayer."*

To Rabbi Sholom Ber Chaikin, for giving selflessly of his valuable time to read, amend, and refine the material, and for ensuring its Halachic accuracy. To Rabbi Shmuel Rabin for proofing the Hebrew text.

To the countless rabbis and lay-leaders who have offered their creative ideas, advice, and never-ending encouragement.

A special thanks to everyone else who helped make this book such a popular staple in homes and synagogues across the globe!

We have devised the following transliteration system to help readers accurately pronounce the Hebrew words of blessings and prayers presented in this book.

Hebrew:	Transliteration:	Example:
כ or ח	ch	Challah
ָ	ö	Of
ַ	a	Hurrah
ֵ	ay	Today
ֶ	e	Leg
ְ	'	Avid
ׂ or וֹ	o	Tone
ִ	i	Key
ֻ or וּ	u	Lunar
י ַ	ai	Aisle
י ָ	öy	Toy

Table of Contents

A Quick Shabbat Primer	7	A Quick Shabbat Primer
Blessings for Candle Lighting	21	בִּרְכוֹת הַדְלָקַת הַנֵּרוֹת
Kiddush for Friday Evening	26	סֵדֶר קִידוּשׁ לְלֵיל שַׁבָּת
Kiddush for Shabbat Day	34	סֵדֶר קִידוּשׁ לְיוֹם הַשַּׁבָּת
Kiddush for Pesach, Shavuot, and Sukkot Eve	39	סֵדֶר קִידוּשׁ לְשָׁלֹשׁ רְגָלִים
Kiddush for the Eve of Rosh Hashana	46	סֵדֶר קִידוּשׁ לְרֹאשׁ הַשָּׁנָה
Kiddush for Festival and Rosh Hashana Day	50	קִידוּשָׁא רַבָּא לְשָׁלֹשׁ רְגָלִים וּלְרֹאשׁ הַשָּׁנָה
Washing the Hands for Bread	52	סֵדֶר נְטִילַת יָדַיִם
Grace After a Meal	54	סֵדֶר בִּרְכַּת הַמָּזוֹן
Grace After a Snack	77	בְּרָכָה אַחֲרוֹנָה
Blessings After a Wedding Meal	82	סֵדֶר שֶׁבַע בְּרָכוֹת
Order of the Third Meal	85	סֵדֶר סְעוּדָה שְׁלִישִׁית
The Havdalah	88	סֵדֶר הַבְדָּלָה
Popular Shabbat Table Songs	91	סֵדֶר נִגּוּנִים

A Quick Shabbat Primer

What is Shabbat?

Shabbat is not just the seventh day of the week or the day on which God rested from creating the world. It is much more than that. Shabbat was made by God as a day unto itself. It has its own identity. It is not just a day meant to be absent of work; unencumbered by our daily distractions, the day of Shabbat is to be used to connect with our spiritual source. Shabbat is also a day on which we stand proudly as Jews, proud to be God's light unto the nations, proud to be the bearers of God's way of life.

We also utilize the Shabbat day to stop, stand back, and appreciate God's creation, and spend time calibrating our "spiritual compass" for the coming week. For the 25 hours of Shabbat we cease interacting with the material world. We stop working and creating, all in order to pause and acknowledge the real Creator, lest we become too self-absorbed in our daily grind to remember that all our fortune comes from God, and realize that our work is only a vessel to receive His bountiful blessings.

On Shabbat we remember our main goal and purpose in this world: we're here not only to achieve fame, accumulate riches, or advance technology, but also to refine the material world we live in.

This is accomplished by following and living by the ways of the Torah, given to us by God, over 3,300 years ago at Mount Sinai. What better way to spend this holy day than with family and friends, immersing ourselves in prayer and Torah study, and maximizing this golden opportunity which comes to us only once a week.

Keeping an Authentic Shabbat

There are many laws and guidelines found in the Torah and Codes of Jewish Law regarding the proper observance of Shabbat. Since Shabbat is God's gift to the Jewish people, we observe it as God wants us to, not merely on our own terms. This means adhering to the proper way Shabbat was practiced by Jews for thousands of years. Many helpful books have been written that explain these laws, and are available in Jewish bookstores. They can help you learn more about the Shabbat and assist you as you embark on this wonderful spiritual journey.

The Message of Shabbat

To obtain a deeper insight into the special nature of Shabbat, what it means to us, and what is its universal message, we will dwell briefly on the main aspects of the Shabbat, particularly those that are reflected in Shabbat prayers.

The Torah tells us that God created the world in six days, and that by the end of the sixth day the heaven and earth and all their hosts were completed. Then God rested from all creative activity, *"and God blessed the seventh day and made it holy."* Thus, right from the beginning of Creation God has set the Shabbat day apart from the other days of the week as a holy day. But for whom was the Shabbat meant? Who was to accept it, appreciate it, and keep it holy? The answer is found in the following meaningful Midrash:

"Rabbi Shimon bar Yochai taught: When God created the holy Shabbat, it said to the Holy One, blessed be He: "Every day You created has a mate. Am I to be the only odd one, without a mate?" Replied God, "The Jewish people will be your mate." And so, while the Jewish people stood at the foot of Mount Sinai to receive the Torah and become a nation, God declared (in the Ten Commandments): "Remember the Shabbat day, to keep it holy!" As if to say, "Remember My promise to the Shabbat that the Jewish nation shall be its mate."

Jewish mystical teachings refer to the Jewish people and the Shabbat in terms of bridegroom and bride, and this is why in the Shabbat prayers, the Shabbat is welcomed with the words, *Bo-i chalöh, Bo-i chalöh* – "Welcome, bride; welcome, bride!" The repetition, *Bo-i chalöh,* alludes to the two great qualities of the "bride," being both "blessed" and "holy," as it is written, "And God blessed the seventh day and made it holy." Indeed, according to Rabbi Yitzchak Arama in his *Akedat Yitzchak*, the word *L'kadsho* – "to keep it holy" – may be rendered "to betroth it," in the sense of *kiddushin,* marriage.

9

In this way, our sages tell us that the Shabbat is uniquely Jewish, that is to say, that the Jewish people and the Shabbat are inseparable; they were destined for each other from the moment of their "birth." Without the Shabbat the Jewish people is simply unthinkable, just as without the Torah, the Jewish people is unthinkable. This is one of the reasons why the Shabbat is equated with all the mitzvot.

Shabbat in the Torah

The origin of the Shabbat, referred to as the Shabbat of Creation, is given in the section of *Vayechulu* in the Bible (see Genesis 2,1), which is also recited during Shabbat services. Shabbat is not mentioned again explicitly in the Torah until after the story of the Exodus, in connection with the manna. This heavenly bread did not come down on the Shabbat, but instead, the children of Israel received a double portion on Friday for Shabbat as well. Then Moses told the children of Israel, *"See, God has given you this Shabbat."*

The Shabbat was nothing new for the children of Israel, for, as our sages tell us, they had known about it traditionally from the time of Abraham and, indeed, observed it even in Egypt. On this occasion, however, they received the first laws about Shabbat, and several weeks later, they received formal instructions on Shabbat in the Ten Commandments at Mount Sinai.

After the Torah was given to our people, the commandment to observe the Shabbat is repeated in the Torah many times with great emphasis. One of the better known passages about the Shabbat is included in the Shabbat morning prayers: *"And the children of Israel shall keep the Shabbat...as an everlasting covenant. It is a sign between Me and the children of Israel forever: That in six days God made heaven and earth, and on the seventh day He ceased from work and rested."*

Here the Torah tells us of the basic significance of the Shabbat as the living sign of God's creation. By keeping the Shabbat, we, the Jewish people, proclaim for the world that God is the Creator of heaven and earth, and we reaffirm the everlasting covenant between God and the Jewish people.

God has crowned His creation with the Shabbat, and has given this crown to us. Our sages of the Talmud expressed it this way, *"A precious gift* —says God— *have I in My treasure stores; its name is Shabbat, and I have given it to you."*

Wearing this crown is, of course, a great privilege. But it also places upon us great responsibilities. These are summed up by Rambam (Maimonides) as follows:

"The Shabbat is the everlasting sign between God and the people of Israel...He who observes the Shabbat properly, honoring it and delighting in it to the best of his ability, is given a reward in this world, over and above the reward that is reserved for him in the World to Come."

Shabbat and Jewish Identity

More than anything else, it has been the Shabbat that has distinguished the Jewish people from all other nations of the world, for Shabbat observance is not just a matter of a single precept or custom, but something that is fundamental to the Jewish religion and Jewish way of life.

During Shabbat, a Jew not only desists from work, closes down his store, factory, or workshop and halts all work at home, but is completely transformed into a person of holiness, devoting the time to prayer and study. Even externally this transformation is in evidence, in one's dress, eating, walking, and talking.

For thousands of years the nations of the world could not understand this Jewish Shabbat. They, who had not known a rest day in the week altogether, thought it deplorable for an entire nation to take off work for a whole day in the week. When Haman complained to King Ahasuerus about the "one people, scattered and dispersed among the nations, whose laws are different from those of any other nation," it was Shabbat and the festivals that he held up to ridicule. Ancient Roman historians called the Jewish people "lazy" and "uncivilized" for their adherence to the Shabbat.

When the nations of the world finally recognized the Torah as a holy book, and called it "The Book" (Bible), they adopted some of its principles. They also introduced a "Sabbath" or "day of rest" into their religions. But it is significant that they made it on Sunday (in

Christianity), or on Friday (in Islam). The Shabbat remained Jewish for Jews alone. Although imitation may be the highest form of flattery, nothing in the imitations can approach the original, Divinely ordained Shabbat, as anyone familiar with the laws of Shabbat and their significance knows.

A Remembrance of the Exodus from Egypt

In the Shabbat sanctification ceremony that we conduct upon arriving home from Friday evening services, known as the Kiddush, we thank God for giving us the Shabbat "as a memorial to the work of Creation" and also "as a remembrance of the Exodus from Egypt." These two basic perceptions of Shabbat are derived from the Ten Commandments, the fourth of which deals with Shabbat.

In the first Decalogue (Exodus 20) it is stated: *"Remember the Shabbat day...for in six days God made heaven and earth, the sea and all that is in them, and ceased work on the seventh day; wherefore God blessed the Shabbat day and sanctified it."* The text in the second Decalogue (Deuteronomy 5) reads: *"Observe the Shabbat day to keep it holy...And you shall remember that you were a slave in the land of Egypt, and God your God brought you out of there by a mighty hand and by an outstretched arm; therefore, God your God commanded you to keep the Shabbat day."*

Commenting on the different aspects of Shabbat as reflected in the Ten Commandments in Exodus and Deuteronomy respectively, the Ramban (Nachmanides) explains that, far from being contradictory, they are supportive and complementary. For as the day of rest attesting to the Creation, Shabbat also brings to mind the time when the Jewish people, being enslaved in Egypt, were not free to rest on that day. They had to work on all seven days of the week. Hence, the Torah emphasizes, *"in order that your manservant and your maidservant may rest as well as you."*

In a deeper sense, the Ramban continues, the Exodus from Egypt confirmed and deepened our belief without doubt in God as Creator of the universe. Until the Exodus from Egypt, the belief in One God came down to the Jewish people from Abraham, Isaac and Jacob, the founders of our Jewish nation, along with the unique covenant that had been established between God and the Patriarchs and their descendants. During the centuries of enslavement, however, belief and tradition were put to severe test.

Many, if not most, of the enslaved Jews must have had some doubts whether there really was a Supreme Being, Creator and Master of the world, or if such a Being had not abandoned the world to its devices, or to the mighty Pharaohs. The Exodus from Egypt, with all its wonders and miracles, demonstrated without any doubt that God was truly the Creator and Master of the world, since He was able at will to suspend and change the laws of nature.

Moreover, the Exodus from Egypt demonstrated, too, that Divine *Hashgachah* ("watchfulness," personal divine providence) extends to every particular and detail of the created order, to humans as well as to the lower orders of animal and plant life, even to the inanimate.

A third essential element of the Exodus experience was the revelation of prophecy. It established the fact that the Creator not only bestowed upon Moses the gift of prophecy, but made him the greatest of all prophets (forty-eight men and seven women, according to our sages). It was at the miraculous crossing of *Yam Suf* (Red Sea; Sea of Reeds) that the liberated Israelites attained complete trust in God and in Moses His servant — meaning, in the prophecy of Moses His servant.

This belief in the truth of Moses' prophecy is no less a cornerstone of our Jewish faith than the belief in the two fundamental principles mentioned above: namely, the existence of a Supreme Being as Creator of the world, and Divine Providence extending to the smallest detail of the created order. For, although the entire nation witnessed the Divine Revelation at Mount Sinai and heard the Decalogue, the entire Torah with all its 613 mitzvot was transmitted through Moses.

In light of the above, the Ramban points out, we can appreciate the Talmudic declaration that "Shabbat equi-balances all the mitzvot," since by keeping Shabbat we attest to the truth of all the fundamental principles of our faith: Creation *ex nihilo*, Divine Providence and Divine Prophecy.

Thus, Ramban concludes, Shabbat is a remembrance of the Exodus from Egypt, while the Exodus from Egypt, in turn, is a memorial to Shabbat of Creation.

Putting Your Best Into Shabbat

Referring to the above-mentioned verse, *"And the children of Israel shall "keep"* (v'sham'ru) *the Shabbat, to "make"* (la-asos) *the Shabbat,"* etc., our sages declare that to "keep" refers to all the laws pertaining to the cessation of work and all that we may not do on Shabbat; and to "make" refers to all things that we have to put into the Shabbat, to honor it, delight in it and fill it with holiness through prayer and study.

Jews make the Shabbat and Shabbat makes the Jewish people. That is what is meant by referring to the Shabbat and the Jewish people as real mates, as mentioned earlier. Indeed, more than the Jewish people kept the Shabbat, the Shabbat has kept the Jewish people, for more than anything else, the Shabbat unites all Jews, in all parts of the world.

The Shabbat is also a reminder to all mankind that it must persistently move toward the "day that is all Shabbat" — a world where all the nations of the world will recognize the sovereignty of the Creator and His rule on earth, a world in which there is no strife, nor violence, nor injustice, for the spirit of Shabbat (peace) will permeate the whole world.

Enjoying a Richly Satisfying Shabbat

A richly satisfying Shabbat never just happens, it is the result of an effort made all week long. The Talmud tells of a sage who purchased all week in honor of Shabbat. Whenever he saw a special food in the market he would buy it and say, "This is for the Shabbat." When he found something better quality, he would replace the earlier item and say, "This is for the Shabbat." Thus, his whole week was permeated with Shabbat!

Now, Shabbat preparations do not only surround food. There are many other preparations that must be done before the onset of the Shabbat at sundown on Friday. For a fuller understanding of these, refer to the Laws of Shabbat section of the "Code of Jewish Law." For introductory purposes, a few of the major points are presented below.

CLOTHING

It is customary to have special clothes for Shabbat. Traditionally this means a white shirt and long dark pants or suit for men and boys, and a modest dress for woman and girls. In fact, many people set aside their nicest suit or dress and wear it only on the Shabbat. In that way, it's obvious to all that Shabbat is a special day.

FOOD

There are three meals eaten on Shabbat. 1) Friday night after the services, 2) Shabbat morning after the services, and 3) late Shabbat afternoon. The table is traditionally decked with a white tablecloth. Some place the Shabbat candles on the dining table (at candle lighting) to enjoy the radiant light of Shabbat during the meal. The finest cutlery, dishes and silverware are also brought out and used.

Among the many traditional foods prepared for the Shabbat, you will find special braided bread called challa, along with dishes of fish, meat, and tasty wines. This is no random selection. This order of foods was handed down to us by our sages, and this precept was extracted from the commandment in the Torah, *"to honor the Shabbat with food and drink."*

Appropriate food for the Shabbat is so important that we are taught that one who cannot afford to purchase any of the above food items, should borrow the money to purchase them!

WORK

As you know by now, Shabbat is a day of rest, and as discussed earlier, this rest is not only a "quiet time," to rejuvenate our energies. While this may also be the case, the rest on Shabbat means the cessation of any creative function we normally do during the week. This is to enable us to recognize and appreciate the One who really does the creating, our God in Heaven.

Practically (and very generally) this means that Jewish people are prohibited from performing any actions associated with the Torah's list of 39 forbidden activities on Shabbat. This includes cooking or lighting fires, driving a car or motorcycle, shopping, handling money, turning lights on or off (lighting a fire), using phones, fax machines, watching TV, going to the movies, playing golf or tennis, sewing, rowing, swimming, skating, boating, flying, barbecuing, etc.

What's left to do?

A Quick Shabbat Primer

A young person came to a Jewish sage and asked, "Why are there so many restrictions on the Shabbat? I feel so imprisoned! I can't watch TV, I can't use the phone, I can't turn on lights, I can't go to the mall."

"Did you hear me say the word prohibited?" the Rabbi asked.

"What do you mean, Rabbi? You taught us that on Shabbat you can't do this and can't do that, and that is how one guards the sanctity of the Shabbat."

The sage replied, "My son, what I said was that on Shabbat you are permitted *not* to watch TV, *not* to answer the phones, *not* to check for email, *not* to cook. You are truly free to rest. This is liberating, not imprisoning!"

Indeed, when was the last time that you felt free to shut out the world and be yourself with your friends, family, and, yes, your Creator? That's what Shabbat is all about! After observing Shabbat and "tuning-out" the world and "tuning-in" to our family and spirituality, you'll feel the happiness, satisfaction, and fulfillment that Shabbat offers everyone who observes it properly.

Our sages relate that Shabbat "takes" from the Friday before and extends into the Saturday night after. We can't just go directly into Shabbat; we have to prepare ourselves beforehand. At the same time, we don't end Shabbat on the dot of sunset on Saturday, but bring some of the Shabbat atmosphere with us into the Saturday evening.

SELF

We spend part of Shabbat day in prayer, a part learning Torah, and a part enjoying the people who are important to us. Shabbat is also an opportune time to do "spiritual accounting." We focus on how we can better ourselves during the week to come.

FAMILY

Shabbat is often called "the glue that keeps the family together." On this day, families spend time eating and sharing thoughts with one another. On Shabbat, it is also customary for parents to learn topics of Jewish values with their children.

Blessings for Candle Lighting

At the appropriate time (see your local Jewish calendar) light the candles (girls light one candle and married women kindle two, adding one for each child). Draw your hands three times around the candles and toward your face. Cover your eyes with your hands, and recite the appropriate blessing.

On Friday Evening

בָּרוּךְ אַתָּה יְיָ, אֱלֹהֵינוּ
מֶלֶךְ הָעוֹלָם, אֲשֶׁר קִדְּשָׁנוּ
בְּמִצְוֹתָיו, וְצִוָּנוּ לְהַדְלִיק
נֵר שֶׁל שַׁבָּת קֹדֶשׁ:

Böruch atöh adonöy, elohaynu
melech hö-olöm, asher kid'shönu
b'mitzvosöv, v'tzivönu l'hadlik
nayr shel shabös kodesh.

Blessed are You, Lord our God, King of the universe, Who has sanctified us with His commandments, and commanded us to kindle the light of the holy Shabbat.

On the Eve of Pesach, Shavuot and Sukkot

בָּרוּךְ אַתָּה יְיָ, אֱלֹהֵינוּ
מֶלֶךְ הָעוֹלָם, אֲשֶׁר קִדְּשָׁנוּ
בְּמִצְוֹתָיו, וְצִוָּנוּ לְהַדְלִיק
נֵר שֶׁל יוֹם טוֹב:

Böruch atöh adonöy, elohaynu
melech hö-olöm, asher kid'shönu
b'mitzvosöv, v'tzivönu l'hadlik
nayr shel yom tov.

Blessed are You, Lord our God, King of the universe, Who has sanctified us with His commandments, and commanded us to kindle the Yom Tov light.

Except on the last two nights of Pesach, continue with:

21

Blessings for Candle Lighting

Böruch atöh adonöy,
elohaynu melech hö-olöm,
she-heche-yönu v'kiy'mönu
v'higi-önu liz'man ha-zeh.

בָּרוּךְ אַתָּה יְיָ,
אֱלֹהֵינוּ מֶלֶךְ הָעוֹלָם,
שֶׁהֶחֱיָנוּ וְקִיְּמָנוּ
וְהִגִּיעָנוּ לִזְמַן הַזֶּה:

Blessed are You, Lord our God, King of the universe, Who has granted us life, sustained us and enabled us to reach this occasion.

On the Eve of Shabbat and Festivals

Böruch atöh adonöy, elohaynu
melech hö-olöm, asher kid'shönu
b'mitzvosöv, v'tzivönu l'hadlik
nayr shel shabös v'shel yom tov.

בָּרוּךְ אַתָּה יְיָ, אֱלֹהֵינוּ
מֶלֶךְ הָעוֹלָם, אֲשֶׁר קִדְּשָׁנוּ
בְּמִצְוֹתָיו, וְצִוָּנוּ לְהַדְלִיק
נֵר שֶׁל שַׁבָּת וְשֶׁל יוֹם טוֹב:

Blessed are You, Lord our God, King of the universe, Who has sanctified us with His commandments, and commanded us to kindle the Shabbat and Yom Tov light.

Except on the last two nights of Pesach, continue with:

Böruch atöh adonöy,
elohaynu melech hö-olöm,
she-heche-yönu v'kiy'mönu
v'higi-önu liz'man ha-zeh.

בָּרוּךְ אַתָּה יְיָ,
אֱלֹהֵינוּ מֶלֶךְ הָעוֹלָם,
שֶׁהֶחֱיָנוּ וְקִיְּמָנוּ
וְהִגִּיעָנוּ לִזְמַן הַזֶּה:

Blessed are You, Lord our God, King of the universe, Who has granted us life, sustained us and enabled us to reach this occasion.

22

Blessings for Candle Lighting

On the Eve of Rosh Hashana

בָּרוּךְ אַתָּה יְיָ, אֱלֹהֵינוּ
מֶלֶךְ הָעוֹלָם, אֲשֶׁר קִדְּשָׁנוּ
בְּמִצְוֹתָיו, וְצִוָּנוּ לְהַדְלִיק
נֵר שֶׁל יוֹם הַזִּכָּרוֹן :

Böruch atöh adonöy, elohaynu
melech hö-olöm, asher kid'shönu
b'mitzvosöv, v'tzivönu l'hadlik
nayr shel yom ha-ziköron.

Blessed are You, Lord our God, King of the universe, Who has sanctified us with His commandments, and commanded us to kindle the light of the Day of Remembrance.

Continue with:

בָּרוּךְ אַתָּה יְיָ,
אֱלֹהֵינוּ מֶלֶךְ הָעוֹלָם,
שֶׁהֶחֱיָנוּ וְקִיְּמָנוּ
וְהִגִּיעָנוּ לִזְמַן הַזֶּה :

Böruch atöh adonöy,
elohaynu melech hö-olöm,
she-heche-yönu v'kiy'mönu
v'higi-önu liz'man ha-zeh.

Blessed are You, Lord our God, King of the universe, Who has granted us life, sustained us and enabled us to reach this occasion.

On the Eve of Rosh Hashana and Shabbat

בָּרוּךְ אַתָּה יְיָ, אֱלֹהֵינוּ
מֶלֶךְ הָעוֹלָם, אֲשֶׁר קִדְּשָׁנוּ
בְּמִצְוֹתָיו, וְצִוָּנוּ לְהַדְלִיק
נֵר שֶׁל שַׁבָּת וְשֶׁל
יוֹם הַזִּכָּרוֹן :

Böruch atöh adonöy, elohaynu
melech hö-olöm, asher kid'shönu
b'mitzvosöv, v'tzivönu l'hadlik
nayr shel shabös v'shel
yom ha-zikoron.

Blessed are You, Lord our God, King of the universe, Who has sanctified us with His commandments, and commanded us to kindle the light of Shabbat and the Day of Remembrance.

23

Blessings for Candle Lighting

Continue with:

Böruch atöh adonöy,
elohaynu melech hö-olöm,
she-heche-yönu v'kiy'mönu
v'higi-önu liz'man ha-zeh.

בָּרוּךְ אַתָּה יְיָ,
אֱלֹהֵינוּ מֶלֶךְ הָעוֹלָם,
שֶׁהֶחֱיָנוּ וְקִיְּמָנוּ
וְהִגִּיעָנוּ לִזְמַן הַזֶּה:

*Blessed are You, Lord our God, King of the universe, Who has granted us
life, sustained us and enabled us to reach this occasion.*

On the Eve of Yom Kippur

Böruch atöh adonöy, elohaynu
melech hö-olöm, asher kid'shönu
b'mitzvosöv, v'tzivönu l'hadlik
nayr shel yom ha-kipurim.

בָּרוּךְ אַתָּה יְיָ, אֱלֹהֵינוּ
מֶלֶךְ הָעוֹלָם, אֲשֶׁר קִדְּשָׁנוּ
בְּמִצְוֹתָיו, וְצִוָּנוּ לְהַדְלִיק
נֵר שֶׁל יוֹם הַכִּפּוּרִים:

*Blessed are You, Lord our God, King of the universe, Who has sanctified us
with His commandments, and commanded us to kindle the Yom Kippur
light.*

Continue with:

Böruch atöh adonöy,
elohaynu melech hö-olöm,
she-heche-yönu v'kiy'mönu
v'higi-önu liz'man ha-zeh.

בָּרוּךְ אַתָּה יְיָ,
אֱלֹהֵינוּ מֶלֶךְ הָעוֹלָם,
שֶׁהֶחֱיָנוּ וְקִיְּמָנוּ
וְהִגִּיעָנוּ לִזְמַן הַזֶּה:

*Blessed are You, Lord our God, King of the universe, Who has granted us
life, sustained us and enabled us to reach this occasion.*

24

Blessings for Candle Lighting

On the Eve of Yom Kippur and Shabbat

Böruch atöh adonöy, elohaynu
melech hö-olöm, asher kid'shönu
b'mitzvosöv, v'tzivönu l'hadlik
nayr shel shabös v'shel
yom ha-kipurim.

בָּרוּךְ אַתָּה יְיָ, אֱלֹהֵינוּ
מֶלֶךְ הָעוֹלָם, אֲשֶׁר קִדְּשָׁנוּ
בְּמִצְוֹתָיו, וְצִוָּנוּ לְהַדְלִיק
נֵר שֶׁל שַׁבָּת וְשֶׁל
יוֹם הַכִּפּוּרִים:

Blessed are You, Lord our God, King of the universe, Who has sanctified us with His commandments, and commanded us to kindle the light of Shabbat and Yom Kippur.

Continue with:

Böruch atöh adonöy,
elohaynu melech hö-olöm,
she-heche-yönu v'kiy'mönu
v'higi-önu liz'man ha-zeh.

בָּרוּךְ אַתָּה יְיָ,
אֱלֹהֵינוּ מֶלֶךְ הָעוֹלָם,
שֶׁהֶחֱיָנוּ וְקִיְּמָנוּ
וְהִגִּיעָנוּ לִזְמַן הַזֶּה:

Blessed are You, Lord our God, King of the universe, Who has granted us life, sustained us and enabled us to reach this occasion.

Kiddush for Friday Evening

Following the Friday evening services, everyone gathers around the table and sings the following verses before the Kiddush is recited. It is customary to have two covered *Challot* (traditional braided bread) on the table at this time.

Shölom alaychem mal-achay
ha-shörays mal-achay el-yon,
mi-melech mal'chay ha-m'löchim
ha-ködosh böruch hu. *Repeat 3 times*

שָׁלוֹם עֲלֵיכֶם מַלְאֲכֵי
הַשָּׁרֵת מַלְאֲכֵי עֶלְיוֹן
מִמֶּלֶךְ מַלְכֵי הַמְּלָכִים
הַקָּדוֹשׁ בָּרוּךְ הוּא : ג"פ

Bo-achem l'shölom mal-achay
ha-shölom mal-achay el-yon,
mi-melech mal'chay ha-m'löchim
ha-ködosh böruch hu. *Repeat 3 times*

בּוֹאֲכֶם לְשָׁלוֹם מַלְאֲכֵי
הַשָּׁלוֹם מַלְאֲכֵי עֶלְיוֹן
מִמֶּלֶךְ מַלְכֵי הַמְּלָכִים
הַקָּדוֹשׁ בָּרוּךְ הוּא : ג"פ

Bö-r'chuni l'shölom mal-achay
ha-shölom mal-achay el-yon,
mi-melech mal'chay ha-m'löchim
ha-ködosh böruch hu. *Repeat 3 times*

בָּרְכוּנִי לְשָׁלוֹם מַלְאֲכֵי
הַשָּׁלוֹם מַלְאֲכֵי עֶלְיוֹן
מִמֶּלֶךְ מַלְכֵי הַמְּלָכִים
הַקָּדוֹשׁ בָּרוּךְ הוּא : ג"פ

Tzays'chem l'shölom mal-achay
ha-shölom mal-achay el-yon,
mi-melech mal'chay ha-m'löchim
ha-ködosh böruch hu. *Repeat 3 times*

צֵאתְכֶם לְשָׁלוֹם מַלְאֲכֵי
הַשָּׁלוֹם מַלְאֲכֵי עֶלְיוֹן
מִמֶּלֶךְ מַלְכֵי הַמְּלָכִים
הַקָּדוֹשׁ בָּרוּךְ הוּא : ג"פ

Kiddush for Friday Evening

Peace unto you, ministering angels, messengers of the Most High, of the supreme King of kings, the Holy One, blessed be He (Say 3 times). May your coming be in peace, angels of peace, messengers of the Most High, of the supreme King of kings, the Holy One, blessed be He (Say 3 times). Bless me with peace, angels of peace, messengers of the Most High, of the supreme King of kings, the Holy One, blessed be He (Say 3 times). May your departure be in peace, angels of peace, messengers of the Most High, of the supreme King of kings, the Holy One, blessed be He (Say 3 times).

Ki mal-öchöv y'tzaveh löch,	כִּי מַלְאָכָיו יְצַוֶּה לָּךְ,
lish-mör'chö b'chöl d'röchechö.	לִשְׁמָרְךָ בְּכָל דְּרָכֶיךָ :
Adonöy yishmör tzays'chö	יְיָ יִשְׁמָר צֵאתְךָ
uvo-echö, may-atöh v'ad olöm.	וּבוֹאֶךָ, מֵעַתָּה וְעַד עוֹלָם :

For He will instruct His angels in your behalf, to guard you in all your ways. The Lord will guard your going and coming from now and for all time.

Ayshes cha-yil mi yimtzö, v'röchok	אֵשֶׁת חַיִל מִי יִמְצָא, וְרָחֹק
mip'ninim michröh. Bötach böh	מִפְּנִינִים מִכְרָהּ : בָּטַח בָּהּ
layv ba-löh, v'shölöl lo yech-sör.	לֵב בַּעְלָהּ, וְשָׁלָל לֹא יֶחְסָר :
G'mölas-hu tov v'lo rö, kol	גְּמָלַתְהוּ טוֹב וְלֹא רָע, כֹּל
y'may cha-yehö. Dö-r'shöh tzemer	יְמֵי חַיֶּיהָ : דָּרְשָׁה צֶמֶר
ufishtim, vata-as b'chayfetz	וּפִשְׁתִּים, וַתַּעַשׂ בְּחֵפֶץ
ka-pehö. Hö-y'söh kö-öniyos	כַּפֶּיהָ : הָיְתָה כָּאֳנִיּוֹת
sochayr, mi-merchök tövi lach-möh.	סוֹחֵר, מִמֶּרְחָק תָּבִיא לַחְמָהּ :
Va-tököm b'od lai-löh, va-titayn teref	וַתָּקָם בְּעוֹד לַיְלָה, וַתִּתֵּן טֶרֶף

27

l'vay-söh, v'chok l'na-arosehö.	לְבֵיתָהּ, וְחֹק לְנַעֲרֹתֶיהָ :
Zö-m'möh sö-deh va-tikö-chayhu,	זָמְמָה שָׂדֶה וַתִּקָּחֵהוּ,
mip'ri chapehö nö-t'öh körem.	מִפְּרִי כַפֶּיהָ נָטְעָה כָּרֶם :
Chö-g'röh b'oz mös-nehö, vat'amaytz	חָגְרָה בְעוֹז מָתְנֶיהָ, וַתְּאַמֵּץ
z'ro-osehö. Tö-amöh ki tov sachröh,	זְרוֹעֹתֶיהָ : טָעֲמָה כִּי טוֹב סַחְרָהּ,
lo yichbeh balai-'löh nayröh.	לֹא יִכְבֶּה בַלַּיְלָה נֵרָהּ :
Yödehö shil'chöh va-kishor,	יָדֶיהָ שִׁלְּחָה בַכִּישׁוֹר,
v'chapehö töm'chu fölech. Kapöh	וְכַפֶּיהָ תָּמְכוּ פָלֶךְ : כַּפָּהּ
pö-r'söh le-öni, v'yödehö shil'chöh	פָּרְשָׂה לֶעָנִי, וְיָדֶיהָ שִׁלְּחָה
lö-ev-yon. Lo sirö l'vaysöh	לָאֶבְיוֹן : לֹא תִירָא לְבֵיתָהּ
mi-shöleg, ki chöl baysöh lövush	מִשָּׁלֶג, כִּי כָל בֵּיתָהּ לָבֻשׁ
shönim. Marvadim ö-s'söh löh,	שָׁנִים : מַרְבַדִּים עָשְׂתָה לָּהּ,
shaysh v'argömön l'vushöh.	שֵׁשׁ וְאַרְגָּמָן לְבוּשָׁהּ :
Nodö bash'örim ba-löh, b'shivto	נוֹדָע בַּשְּׁעָרִים בַּעְלָהּ, בְּשִׁבְתּוֹ
im zik'nay öretz. Södin ö-s'söh	עִם זִקְנֵי אָרֶץ : סָדִין עָשְׂתָה
va-timkor, va-chagor nö-s'nöh	וַתִּמְכֹּר, וַחֲגוֹר נָתְנָה
lak'na-ani. Oz v'hödör	לַכְּנַעֲנִי : עוֹז וְהָדָר
l'vushöh, va-tis-chak l'yom acharon.	לְבוּשָׁהּ, וַתִּשְׂחַק לְיוֹם אַחֲרוֹן :
Pihö pö-s'chöh v'chöchmöh, v'soras	פִּיהָ פָּתְחָה בְחָכְמָה, וְתוֹרַת
chesed al l'shonöh. Tzofiyöh	חֶסֶד עַל לְשׁוֹנָהּ : צוֹפִיָּה
ha-lichos baysöh, v'lechem atz-lus	הֲלִיכוֹת בֵּיתָהּ, וְלֶחֶם עַצְלוּת
lo sochayl. Kömu vönehö	לֹא תֹאכֵל : קָמוּ בָנֶיהָ
va-y'ash'ruhö, ba-löh va-y'ha-l'löh.	וַיְאַשְּׁרוּהָ, בַּעְלָהּ וַיְהַלְלָהּ :
Rabos bönos ösu chö-yil, v'at ölis	רַבּוֹת בָּנוֹת עָשׂוּ חָיִל, וְאַתְּ עָלִית

al kulönöh. Sheker ha-chayn v'hevel
ha-yofi, ishöh yir'as adonöy hi
sis-halöl. T'nu löh mip'ri yödehö,
viha-l'luhö bash'örim ma-asehö.

עַל כֻּלָּנָה: שֶׁקֶר הַחֵן וְהֶבֶל
הַיֹּפִי, אִשָּׁה יִרְאַת יְיָ הִיא
תִתְהַלָּל: תְּנוּ לָהּ מִפְּרִי יָדֶיהָ,
וִיהַלְלוּהָ בַשְּׁעָרִים מַעֲשֶׂיהָ:

Who can find a wife of excellence? Her value far exceeds that of gems. The heart of her husband trusts in her; he lacks no gain. She treats him with goodness, never with evil, all the days of her life. She seeks out wool and flax, and works willingly with her hands. She is like the merchant ships; she brings her food from afar. She rises while it is still night, gives food to her household, and sets out the tasks for her maids. She considers a field and buys it; from her earnings she plants a vineyard. She girds her loins with strength, and flexes her arms. She realizes that her enterprise is profitable; her lamp does not go out at night. She puts her hands on the spindle, and her palms grasp the distaff. She holds out her hand to the poor, and extends her hands to the destitute. She does not fear for her household in the frost, for her entire household is clothed [warmly] in scarlet. She makes her own tapestries; her garments are of fine linen and purple. Her husband is well-known at the gates, as he sits with the elders of the land. She makes linens and sells [them]; she provides the merchants with girdles. Strength and dignity are her garb; she looks smilingly toward the future. She opens her mouth with wisdom, and the teaching of kindness is on her tongue. She watches the conduct of her household, and does not eat the bread of idleness. Her children rise and acclaim her, her husband—and he praises her: Many daughters have done worthily, but you surpass them all. Charm is deceptive and beauty is naught; a God-fearing woman is the one to be praised. Give her praise for her accomplishments, and let her deeds laud her at the gates.

Kiddush for Friday Evening

Mizmor l'dövid, adonöy ro-i lo ech-sör. Bin'os deshe yarbi-tzayni, al may m'nuchos y'nahalayni. Nafshi y'shovayv, yan-chayni v'ma-g'lay tzedek l'ma-an sh'mo. Gam ki ay-laych b'gay tzal-möves lo irö rö, ki atöh imödi, shiv-t'chö umish-antechö hay-möh y'nachamuni. Ta-aroch l'fönai shulchön neged tzo-r'röy, dishan-tö va-shemen roshi, kosi r'vö-yöh. Ach tov vöchesed yir-d'funi köl y'may cha-yöy, v'shavti b'vays adonöy l'orech yömim.

מִזְמוֹר לְדָוִד, יְיָ רֹעִי לֹא
אֶחְסָר : בִּנְאוֹת דֶּשֶׁא יַרְבִּיצֵנִי, עַל
מֵי מְנוּחוֹת יְנַהֲלֵנִי : נַפְשִׁי
יְשׁוֹבֵב, יַנְחֵנִי בְמַעְגְּלֵי
צֶדֶק לְמַעַן שְׁמוֹ : גַּם כִּי
אֵלֵךְ בְּגֵיא צַלְמָוֶת לֹא אִירָא רָע,
כִּי אַתָּה עִמָּדִי, שִׁבְטְךָ
וּמִשְׁעַנְתֶּךָ הֵמָּה
יְנַחֲמֻנִי : תַּעֲרֹךְ לְפָנַי
שֻׁלְחָן נֶגֶד צֹרְרָי, דִּשַּׁנְתָּ
בַשֶּׁמֶן רֹאשִׁי, כּוֹסִי רְוָיָה : אַךְ
טוֹב וָחֶסֶד יִרְדְּפוּנִי כָּל יְמֵי
חַיָּי, וְשַׁבְתִּי בְּבֵית יְיָ
לְאֹרֶךְ יָמִים :

A Psalm by David. The Lord is my shepherd; I shall lack nothing. He makes me lie down in green pastures; He leads me beside still waters. He revives my soul; He directs me in the paths of righteousness for the sake of His Name. Even if I walk in the valley of the shadow of death, I will fear no evil, for You are with me; Your rod and Your staff – they will comfort me. You will prepare a table before my enemies; You have anointed my head with oil; my cup is full. Only goodness and kindness shall follow me all the days of my life, and I shall dwell in the House of the Lord for many long years.

Kiddush for Friday Evening

Dö hi s'udöső da-chakal	דָּא הִיא סְעוּדָתָא דַּחֲקַל
ta-puchin kadishin.	תַּפּוּחִין קַדִּישִׁין :

This is the meal of the holy "Chakal Tapuchin" (ed.: Kabbalistic term for a manifestation of God's presence).

Askinu s'udöső dim'hay-m'nusö	אַתְקִינוּ סְעוּדָתָא דִמְהֵימְנוּתָא
sh'laymöső chedvöső d'malkö	שְׁלֵמָתָא חֶדְוָתָא דְמַלְכָּא
ka-dishö. Askinu s'udöső d'malkö	קַדִּישָׁא. אַתְקִינוּ סְעוּדָתָא דְמַלְכָּא
dö hi s'udöső da-chakal ta-puchin	דָּא הִיא סְעוּדָתָא דַּחֲקַל תַּפּוּחִין
ka-dishin, uz'ayr anpin v'atikö	קַדִּישִׁין, וּזְעֵר אַנְפִּין וְעַתִּיקָא
ka-dishö asyön l'sa-adö ba-hadöh.	קַדִּישָׁא אַתְיָן לְסַעֲדָא בַּהֲדַהּ :

Prepare the meal of perfect faith, which is the delight of the holy King; prepare the meal of the King. This is the meal of the holy "Chakal Tapuchin," and Z'eir Anpin and the holy Ancient One come to join her in the meal.

Directions for the Kiddush

The Kiddush is recited standing, while holding a cup of wine or grape juice containing at least 3.5 fluid ounces. Fill the cup and lift it with your right hand, then transfer it to the left hand. Now lower it into the cupped palm of your right hand (if you write with your left hand, reverse). Lift the cup at least 10 inches above the table. Recite the passages and blessings below.

Kiddush for Friday Evening

Yom ha-shishi. Va-y'chulu ha-shöma-yim v'hö-öretz v'chöl tz'vö-öm. Va-y'chal elohim ba-yom ha-sh'vi-i, m'lachto asher ösöh, va-yishbos ba-yom ha-sh'vi-i miköl m'lachto asher ösöh. Va-y'vörech elohim es yom ha-sh'vi-i, va-y'kadaysh oso, ki vo shövas miköl m'lachto, asher börö elohim la-asos.

יוֹם הַשִּׁשִּׁי : וַיְכֻלּוּ הַשָּׁמַיִם וְהָאָרֶץ וְכָל צְבָאָם : וַיְכַל אֱלֹהִים בַּיּוֹם הַשְּׁבִיעִי, מְלַאכְתּוֹ אֲשֶׁר עָשָׂה, וַיִּשְׁבֹּת בַּיּוֹם הַשְּׁבִיעִי מִכָּל מְלַאכְתּוֹ אֲשֶׁר עָשָׂה : וַיְבָרֶךְ אֱלֹהִים אֶת יוֹם הַשְּׁבִיעִי, וַיְקַדֵּשׁ אֹתוֹ, כִּי בוֹ שָׁבַת מִכָּל מְלַאכְתּוֹ, אֲשֶׁר בָּרָא אֱלֹהִים לַעֲשׂוֹת :

The sixth day. And the heavens and the earth and all their hosts were completed. And God finished by the Seventh Day His work which He had done, and He rested on the Seventh Day from all His work which He had done. And God blessed the Seventh Day and made it holy, for on it He rested from all His work which God created to function.

Savri mörönön: Böruch atöh adonöy elohaynu melech hö-olöm, boray p'ri ha-göfen.

סַבְרִי מָרָנָן : בָּרוּךְ אַתָּה יְיָ אֱלֹהֵינוּ מֶלֶךְ הָעוֹלָם, בּוֹרֵא פְּרִי הַגָּפֶן :

Attention, gentlemen! Blessed are You, Lord our God, King of the universe, Who creates the fruit of the vine.

Böruch atöh adonöy elohaynu melech hö-olöm, asher kid'shönu b'mitzvosöv v'rötzöh bönu,

בָּרוּךְ אַתָּה יְיָ אֱלֹהֵינוּ מֶלֶךְ הָעוֹלָם, אֲשֶׁר קִדְּשָׁנוּ בְּמִצְוֹתָיו וְרָצָה בָנוּ,

32

v'shabas köd-sho b'ahavöh	וְשַׁבַּת קָדְשׁוֹ בְּאַהֲבָה
uv'rötzon hin-chilönu, ziköron	וּבְרָצוֹן הִנְחִילָנוּ, זִכָּרוֹן
l'ma-asay v'rayshis, t'chilöh	לְמַעֲשֵׂה בְרֵאשִׁית, תְּחִלָּה
l'mikrö-ay kodesh, zaycher li-tzi-as	לְמִקְרָאֵי קֹדֶשׁ, זֵכֶר לִיצִיאַת
mitzrö-yim. Ki vönu vöchartö,	מִצְרָיִם. כִּי בָנוּ בָחַרְתָּ,
v'osönu kidashtö miköl hö-amim.	וְאוֹתָנוּ קִדַּשְׁתָּ מִכָּל הָעַמִּים.
V'shabas köd-sh'chö b'ahavöh	וְשַׁבַּת קָדְשְׁךָ בְּאַהֲבָה
uv'rötzon hin-chaltönu. Böruch	וּבְרָצוֹן הִנְחַלְתָּנוּ. בָּרוּךְ
atöh adonöy, m'kadaysh ha-shabös.	אַתָּה יְיָ מְקַדֵּשׁ הַשַּׁבָּת:

Blessed are You, Lord our God, King of the universe, Who has hallowed us with His commandments, has desired us, and has given us, in love and goodwill, His holy Shabbat as a heritage, in remembrance of the work of creation; the first of the holy Festivals, commemorating the Exodus from Egypt. For You have chosen us and sanctified us from among all the nations, and with love and goodwill given us Your holy Shabbat as a heritage. Blessed are You Lord, Who hallows the Shabbat.

During Sukkot add:	בסוכות:
Böruch atöh adonöy elohaynu	בָּרוּךְ אַתָּה יְיָ אֱלֹהֵינוּ
melech hö-olöm, asher kid'shönu	מֶלֶךְ הָעוֹלָם, אֲשֶׁר קִדְּשָׁנוּ
b'mitzvosöv v'tzivönu	בְּמִצְוֹתָיו וְצִוָּנוּ
lay-shayv ba-suköh.	לֵישֵׁב בַּסֻּכָּה:

Blessed are You, Lord our God, King of the universe, Who has sanctified us with His commandments, and commanded us to dwell in the Sukkah.

Sit down and drink at least two ounces. Distribute some wine to everyone present. Proceed with the washing of the hands for bread (p. 52).

Kiddush for Shabbat Day

Mizmor l'dövid, adonöy ro-i lo ech-sör. Bin'os deshe yarbi-tzayni, al may m'nuchos y'nahalayni. Nafshi y'shovayv, yan-chayni v'ma-g'lay tzedek l'ma-an sh'mo. Gam ki ay-laych b'gay tzal-möves lo irö rö, ki atöh imödi, shiv-t'chö umish-antechö hay-möh y'na-chamuni. Ta-aroch l'fönai shulchön neged tzo-r'röy, dishan-tö va-shemen roshi, kosi r'vö-yöh. Ach tov vö-chesed yir-d'funi köl y'may cha-yöy, v'shavti b'vays adonöy l'orech yömim.

מִזְמוֹר לְדָוִד, יְיָ רֹעִי לֹא אֶחְסָר : בִּנְאוֹת דֶּשֶׁא יַרְבִּיצֵנִי, עַל מֵי מְנוּחוֹת יְנַהֲלֵנִי : נַפְשִׁי יְשׁוֹבֵב, יַנְחֵנִי בְמַעְגְּלֵי צֶדֶק לְמַעַן שְׁמוֹ : גַּם כִּי אֵלֵךְ בְּגֵיא צַלְמָוֶת לֹא אִירָא רָע, כִּי אַתָּה עִמָּדִי, שִׁבְטְךָ וּמִשְׁעַנְתֶּךָ הֵמָּה יְנַחֲמֻנִי : תַּעֲרֹךְ לְפָנַי שֻׁלְחָן נֶגֶד צֹרְרָי, דִּשַּׁנְתָּ בַשֶּׁמֶן רֹאשִׁי, כּוֹסִי רְוָיָה : אַךְ טוֹב וָחֶסֶד יִרְדְּפוּנִי כָּל יְמֵי חַיָּי, וְשַׁבְתִּי בְּבֵית יְיָ לְאֹרֶךְ יָמִים :

A Psalm by David. The Lord is my shepherd; I shall lack nothing. He makes me lie down in green pastures; He leads me beside still waters. He revives my soul; He directs me in the paths of righteousness for the sake of His Name. Even if I walk in the valley of the shadow of death, I will fear no evil, for You are with me; Your rod and Your staff — they will comfort me. You will prepare a table before my enemies; You have anointed my head with oil; my cup is full. Only goodness and kindness shall follow me all the days of my life, and I shall dwell in the House of the Lord for many long years.

34

Kiddush for Shabbat Day

Askinu s'udösö dim'hay-m'nusö
sh'laymösö ched-vösö d'malkö
ka-dishö. Askinu s'udösö d'malkö,
dö hi s'udöso d'atikö ka-dishö,
va-chakal ta-puchin ka-dishin uz'ayr
anpin asyön l'sa-adö ba-hadayh.

אַתְקִינוּ סְעוּדָתָא דִמְהֵימְנוּתָא
שְׁלֵמָתָא חֶדְוָתָא דְמַלְכָּא
קַדִּישָׁא, אַתְקִינוּ סְעוּדָתָא דְמַלְכָּא,
דָּא הִיא סְעוּדָתָא דְעַתִּיקָא קַדִּישָׁא,
וַחֲקַל תַּפּוּחִין קַדִּישִׁין וּזְעֵר
אַנְפִּין אַתְיָן לְסַעֲדָא בַּהֲדֵיהּ:

Prepare the meal of perfect faith, which is the delight of the holy King; prepare the meal of the King. This is the meal of the the holy Ancient One, and the holy "Chakal Tapuchin," and "Zeir Anpin" come to join Him in the meal (ed.: Kabbalistic terms for manifestations of God's presence).

V'shöm'ru v'nay yisrö-ayl es
ha-shabös, la-asos es ha-shabös
l'dorosöm b'ris olöm. Bayni uvayn
b'nay yisrö-ayl os hi l'olöm,
ki shay-shes yömim ösöh adonöy es
ha-shöma-yim v'es hö-öretz
uva-yom ha-sh'vi-i
shövas va-yinöfash.

וְשָׁמְרוּ בְנֵי יִשְׂרָאֵל אֶת
הַשַּׁבָּת, לַעֲשׂוֹת אֶת הַשַּׁבָּת
לְדֹרֹתָם בְּרִית עוֹלָם. בֵּינִי וּבֵין
בְּנֵי יִשְׂרָאֵל אוֹת הִיא לְעֹלָם,
כִּי שֵׁשֶׁת יָמִים עָשָׂה יְיָ אֶת
הַשָּׁמַיִם וְאֶת הָאָרֶץ,
וּבַיּוֹם הַשְּׁבִיעִי
שָׁבַת וַיִּנָּפַשׁ:

And the children of Israel shall observe the Shabbat, establishing the Shabbat throughout their generations as an everlasting covenant. It is a sign between Me and the children of Israel for all time, for in six days the Lord made the heavens and the earth, and on the seventh day He ceased from work and rested.

Kiddush for Shabbat Day

Im töshiv mi-shabös rag-lechö,
asos chafö-tzechö b'yom köd-shi,
v'körö-sö la-shabös oneg, lik'dosh
adonöy m'chuböd, v'chibad-to
may-asos d'röchechö mim'tzo
chef-tz'chö v'dabayr dövör. Öz
tis-anag al adonöy, v'hirkav-tichö al
bömösay öretz, v'ha-achal-tichö
nacha-las ya-akov övichö,
ki pi adonöy dibayr.

אִם תָּשִׁיב מִשַּׁבָּת רַגְלֶךָ,
עֲשׂוֹת חֲפָצֶךָ בְּיוֹם קָדְשִׁי,
וְקָרָאתָ לַשַּׁבָּת עֹנֶג, לִקְדוֹשׁ
יְיָ מְכֻבָּד, וְכִבַּדְתּוֹ
מֵעֲשׂוֹת דְּרָכֶיךָ מִמְּצוֹא
חֶפְצְךָ וְדַבֵּר דָּבָר. אָז
תִּתְעַנַּג עַל יְיָ, וְהִרְכַּבְתִּיךָ עַל
בָּמֳתֵי אָרֶץ, וְהַאֲכַלְתִּיךָ
נַחֲלַת יַעֲקֹב אָבִיךָ,
כִּי פִּי יְיָ דִּבֵּר:

If you restrain your feet because of the Shabbat from attending to your affairs on My holy day, and you call the Shabbat, "delight," the day made holy by the Lord, "honored," and you honor it by not following your customary ways, refraining from pursuing your affairs and from speaking profane things, then you shall delight in the Lord, and I will make you ride on the high places of the earth, and I will nourish you with the heritage of Jacob your father; thus the mouth of the Lord has spoken.

Dö hi s'udösö d'atikö ka-dishö.
דָּא הִיא סְעוּדָתָא דְּעַתִּיקָא קַדִּישָׁא:

This is the meal of the holy Ancient One.

Kiddush for Shabbat Day

Zöchor es yom ha-shabös l'ka-d'sho.	זָכוֹר אֶת יוֹם הַשַּׁבָּת לְקַדְּשׁוֹ.
Shay-shes yömim ta-avod v'ösisö	שֵׁשֶׁת יָמִים תַּעֲבֹד וְעָשִׂיתָ
köl m'lach-techö. V'yom ha-sh'vi-i	כָּל מְלַאכְתֶּךָ. וְיוֹם הַשְּׁבִיעִי
shabös la-donöy elo-hechö, lo	שַׁבָּת לַיְיָ אֱלֹהֶיךָ, לֹא
sa-aseh chöl m'löchöh, atöh	תַעֲשֶׂה כָל מְלָאכָה, אַתָּה
uvin'chö uvitechö av-d'chö	וּבִנְךָ וּבִתֶּךָ עַבְדְּךָ
va-amös'chö uv'hemtechö,	וַאֲמָתְךָ וּבְהֶמְתֶּךָ,
v'gayr'chö asher bish'örechö.	וְגֵרְךָ אֲשֶׁר בִּשְׁעָרֶיךָ.
Ki shayshes yömim ösöh adonöy	כִּי שֵׁשֶׁת יָמִים עָשָׂה יְיָ
es ha-shöma-yim v'es hö-öretz,	אֶת הַשָּׁמַיִם וְאֶת הָאָרֶץ,
es ha-yöm v'es köl asher böm,	אֶת הַיָּם וְאֶת כָּל אֲשֶׁר בָּם,
va-yönach ba-yom ha-sh'vi-i,	וַיָּנַח בַּיּוֹם הַשְּׁבִיעִי,

Remember the Shabbat day to sanctify it. Six days you shall labor, and do all your work, but the seventh day is Shabbat for the Lord your God; you shall not do any work — you, your son or your daughter, your manservant or your maidservant, or your cattle, or the stranger within your gates. For [in] six days the Lord made the heavens, the earth, the sea, and all that is in them, and rested on the seventh day...

Directions for the Kiddush

The Kiddush is recited standing, while holding a cup of wine or grape juice containing at least 3.5 fluid ounces. Fill the cup and lift it with your right hand, then transfer it to the left hand. Now lower it into the cupped palm of

Kiddush for Shabbat Day

your right hand (if you write with your left hand, reverse). Lift the cup at least 10 inches above the table. Recite the passage and blessing below.

Al kayn bay-rach adonöy עַל כֵּן בֵּרַךְ יְיָ
es yom ha-shabös אֶת יוֹם הַשַּׁבָּת
va-y'kad'shayhu. וַיְקַדְּשֵׁהוּ:

...therefore the Lord blessed the Shabbat day and made it holy.

Savri mörönön: Böruch atöh adonöy סַבְרִי מָרָנָן: בָּרוּךְ אַתָּה יְיָ
elohaynu melech hö-olöm, אֱלֹהֵינוּ מֶלֶךְ הָעוֹלָם,
boray p'ri ha-göfen. בּוֹרֵא פְּרִי הַגָּפֶן:

Attention, gentlemen! Blessed are You, Lord our God, King of the universe, Who creates the fruit of the vine.

During Sukkot add: בסוכות:
Böruch atöh adonöy elohaynu בָּרוּךְ אַתָּה יְיָ אֱלֹהֵינוּ
melech hö-olöm, asher kid'shönu מֶלֶךְ הָעוֹלָם, אֲשֶׁר קִדְּשָׁנוּ
b'mitzvosöv v'tzivonu בְּמִצְוֹתָיו וְצִוָּנוּ
layshayv ba-suköh. לֵישֵׁב בַּסֻּכָּה:

Blessed are You, Lord our God, King of the universe, Who has sanctified us with His commandments, and commanded us to dwell in the Sukkah.

Sit down and drink at least two ounces. Distribute some wine to everyone present. Proceed with the washing of the hands for bread (p. 52).

Kiddush for Pesach, Shavuot, & Sukkot Eve

If the Festival occurs on a weekday, begin with *Askinu S'udösö* (below), then skip to *Savri Moronon*. If the Festival occurs on Shabbat, recite quietly from *Shölöm Alaychem* until *Yom Hashishi* (pp. 26-31), then resume below from *Yom Hashishi*, and include all parenthesized words in the blessings.

Askinu s'udösö d'malkö	אַתְקִינוּ סְעוּדָתָא דְּמַלְכָּא
ilö-öh, dö hi s'udösö d'kud-shö	עִלָּאָה, דָּא הִיא סְעוּדָתָא דְּקוּדְשָׁא
b'rich hu ush'chintayh.	בְּרִיךְ הוּא וּשְׁכִינְתֵּיה:

Prepare the meal of the supernal King. This is the meal of the Holy One, blessed be He, and His Shechinah (ed.: Kabbalistic term for a manifestation of God's presence).

Directions for the Kiddush

The Kiddush is recited standing, while holding a cup of wine or grape juice containing at least 3.5 fluid ounces. Fill the cup and lift it with your right hand, then transfer it to the left hand. Now lower it into the cupped palm of your right hand (if you write with your left hand, reverse). Lift the cup at least 10 inches above the table. Recite the passages and blessings below.

On Shabbat begin here:

Yom ha-shishi. Va-y'chulu
ha-shöma-yim v'hö-öretz v'chöl
tz'vö-öm. Va-y'chal elohim ba-yom
ha-sh'vi-i, m'lachto asher ösöh,
va-yishbos ba-yom ha-sh'vi-i miköl
m'lachto asher ösöh. Va-y'vörech
elohim es yom ha-sh'vi-i,
va-y'kadaysh oso, ki vo shövas
miköl m'lachto, asher börö
elohim la-asos. **Continue below**

יוֹם הַשִּׁשִׁי : וַיְכֻלּוּ
הַשָּׁמַיִם וְהָאָרֶץ וְכָל
צְבָאָם : וַיְכַל אֱלֹהִים בַּיּוֹם
הַשְּׁבִיעִי, מְלַאכְתּוֹ אֲשֶׁר עָשָׂה,
וַיִּשְׁבֹּת בַּיּוֹם הַשְּׁבִיעִי מִכָּל
מְלַאכְתּוֹ אֲשֶׁר עָשָׂה : וַיְבָרֶךְ
אֱלֹהִים אֶת יוֹם הַשְּׁבִיעִי,
וַיְקַדֵּשׁ אֹתוֹ, כִּי בוֹ שָׁבַת
מִכָּל מְלַאכְתּוֹ, אֲשֶׁר בָּרָא
אֱלֹהִים לַעֲשׂוֹת :

The sixth day. And the heavens and the earth and all their hosts were completed. And God finished by the Seventh Day His work which He had done, and He rested on the Seventh Day from all His work which He had done. And God blessed the Seventh Day and made it holy, for on it He rested from all His work which God created to function.

During the week begin here:

Savri mörönön: Böruch atöh adonöy
elohaynu melech hö-olöm,
boray p'ri ha-göfen.

סַבְרִי מָרָנָן : בָּרוּךְ אַתָּה יְיָ
אֱלֹהֵינוּ מֶלֶךְ הָעוֹלָם,
בּוֹרֵא פְּרִי הַגָּפֶן :

Attention, gentlemen! Blessed are You, Lord our God, King of the universe, Who creates the fruit of the vine.

40

Böruch atöh adonöy elohaynu בָּרוּךְ אַתָּה יְיָ אֱלֹהֵינוּ

melech hö-olöm, asher böchar bönu מֶלֶךְ הָעוֹלָם, אֲשֶׁר בָּחַר בָּנוּ

miköl öm v'ro-m'mönu miköl löshon מִכָּל עָם וְרוֹמְמָנוּ מִכָּל לָשׁוֹן

v'kid'shönu b'mitzvosöv, va-titen וְקִדְּשָׁנוּ בְּמִצְוֹתָיו, וַתִּתֶּן

lönu adonöy elohaynu b'ahavöh לָנוּ יְיָ אֱלֹהֵינוּ בְּאַהֲבָה

(shabösos lim'nuchöh u-) (שַׁבָּתוֹת לִמְנוּחָה וּ)

mo-adim l'simchöh cha-gim מוֹעֲדִים לְשִׂמְחָה חַגִּים

uz'manim l'söson es yom וּזְמַנִּים לְשָׂשׂוֹן אֶת יוֹם

(ha-shabös ha-zeh v'es yom) (הַשַּׁבָּת הַזֶּה וְאֶת יוֹם)

On Pesach: לפסח:

chag ha-matzos ha-zeh... ...חַג הַמַּצּוֹת הַזֶּה

On Shavuot: לשבועות:

chag ha-shövu-os ha-zeh... ...חַג הַשָּׁבוּעוֹת הַזֶּה

On Sukkot: לסוכות:

chag ha-sukos ha-zeh... ...חַג הַסֻּכּוֹת הַזֶּה

On Shmini Atzeret and לשמיני עצרת

Simchat Torah: ולשמחת תורה:

sh'mini atzeres ha-chag ha-zeh... ...שְׁמִינִי עֲצֶרֶת הַחַג הַזֶּה

Continue here:

...v'es yom tov mikrö kodesh וְאֶת יוֹם טוֹב מִקְרָא קֹדֶשׁ...

ha-zeh, z'man... ...הַזֶּה, זְמַן

On Pesach: לפסח:

chay-rusaynu... ...חֵרוּתֵנוּ

41

Kiddush for Pesach, Shavuot, & Sukkot Eve

On Shavuot:	לשבועות:
matan torö-saynu...	מַתַּן תּוֹרָתֵנוּ...
On Sukkot:	לסוכות:
simchö-saynu...	שִׂמְחָתֵנוּ...
On Shmini Atzeret and Simchat Torah:	לשמיני עצרת ולשמחת תורה:
simchö-saynu...	שִׂמְחָתֵנוּ...

...(b'ahavöh) mikrö kodesh zaycher litzi-as mitzrö-yim, ki vönu vöchartö v'osönu kidashtö miköl hö-amim, (v'shabös) umo-aday köd-shechö (b'ahavöh uv'rötzon) b'simchöh uv'söson hin-chaltönu. Böruch atöh adonöy m'kadaysh (ha-shabös v') yisrö-ayl v'haz'manim.

...(בְּאַהֲבָה) מִקְרָא קֹדֶשׁ זֵכֶר לִיצִיאַת מִצְרָיִם, כִּי בָנוּ בָחַרְתָּ וְאוֹתָנוּ קִדַּשְׁתָּ מִכָּל הָעַמִּים, (וְשַׁבָּת) וּמוֹעֲדֵי קָדְשֶׁךָ (בְּאַהֲבָה וּבְרָצוֹן) בְּשִׂמְחָה וּבְשָׂשׂוֹן הִנְחַלְתָּנוּ: בָּרוּךְ אַתָּה יְיָ מְקַדֵּשׁ (הַשַּׁבָּת וְ) יִשְׂרָאֵל וְהַזְּמַנִּים:

On Saturday night continue with the Festival Havdalah (p. 44).

On Saturday night continue with the Festival Havdalah (p. 44).

During Sukkot add:	בסוכות:

Böruch atöh adonöy elohaynu melech hö-olöm, asher kid'shönu b'mitzvosöv v'tzivönu layshayv ba-suköh.

בָּרוּךְ אַתָּה יְיָ אֱלֹהֵינוּ מֶלֶךְ הָעוֹלָם, אֲשֶׁר קִדְּשָׁנוּ בְּמִצְוֹתָיו וְצִוָּנוּ לֵישֵׁב בַּסֻּכָּה:

Kiddush for Pesach, Shavuot, & Sukkot Eve

Blessed are You, Lord our God, King of the universe, Who has sanctified us with His commandments, and commanded us to dwell in the Sukkah.

On the second night of Sukkot, the following blessing is recited before the previous one. This blessing is omitted on the last days of Pesach.

Böruch atöh adonöy, elohaynu   בָּרוּךְ אַתָּה יְיָ אֱלֹהֵינוּ

melech hö-olöm, she-heche-yönu   מֶלֶךְ הָעוֹלָם, שֶׁהֶחֱיָנוּ

v'kiy'mönu v'higi-önu   וְקִיְּמָנוּ וְהִגִּיעָנוּ

liz'man ha-zeh.   לִזְמַן הַזֶּה:

Blessed are You, Lord our God, King of the universe, Who has chosen us from among all nations, raised us above all tongues, and made us holy through His commandments. And You, Lord our God, have given us in love (on Shabbat: Sabbaths for rest and) Festivals for rejoicing, holidays and seasons for gladness, (on Shabbat: this Shabbat day and) this day of: (on Pesach: the Festival of Matzot, and this Festival of holy assembly, the season of our freedom), (on Shavuot: the Festival of Shavuot, and this Festival of holy assembly, the season of the giving of our Torah), (on Sukkot: the Festival of Sukkot, and this Festival of holy assembly, the season of our rejoicing), (on Shmini Atzeret and Simchat Torah: Shmini Atzeret and this Festival of holy assembly, the season of our rejoicing,) (on Shabbat: in love,) a holy assembly, commemorating the Exodus from Egypt. For You have chosen us and sanctified us from among all the nations, and Your holy (on Shabbat: Shabbat and) Festivals (on Shabbat: in love and goodwill), in joy and gladness, You have given us as a heritage. Blessed are You Lord, Who sanctifies (on Shabbat: the Shabbat and) Israel and the [festive] seasons. Blessed are you, Lord our God, King of the universe, Who has granted us life, sustained us and enabled us to reach this occasion.

Sit down and drink at least two ounces. Distribute some wine to everyone present. Proceed with the washing of the hands for bread (p. 52).

Havdalah for when the Festival falls on Saturday night

Recited on a flame: Böruch atöh adonöy elohaynu melech hö-olöm, boray m'oray hö-aysh. **Look at the flame.**

בָּרוּךְ אַתָּה יְיָ אֱלֹהֵינוּ מֶלֶךְ הָעוֹלָם, בּוֹרֵא מְאוֹרֵי הָאֵשׁ.

Böruch atöh adonöy elohaynu melech hö-olöm, ha-mavdil bayn kodesh l'chol, bayn or l'cho-shech, bayn yisrö-ayl lö-amim, bayn yom ha-sh'vi-i l'shay-shes y'may ha-ma-aseh. Bayn k'dushas shabös lik'dushas yom tov hiv-daltö, v'es yom ha-sh'vi-i mi-shay-shes y'may ha-ma-aseh ki-dash-tö, hivdaltö v'kidash-tö es am'chö yisrö-ayl bik'dushö-sechö. Böruch atöh adonöy, ha-mavdil bayn kodesh l'kodesh.

בָּרוּךְ אַתָּה יְיָ אֱלֹהֵינוּ מֶלֶךְ הָעוֹלָם, הַמַּבְדִּיל בֵּין קֹדֶשׁ לְחוֹל, בֵּין אוֹר לְחֹשֶׁךְ, בֵּין יִשְׂרָאֵל לָעַמִּים, בֵּין יוֹם הַשְּׁבִיעִי לְשֵׁשֶׁת יְמֵי הַמַּעֲשֶׂה. בֵּין קְדֻשַּׁת שַׁבָּת לִקְדֻשַּׁת יוֹם טוֹב הִבְדַּלְתָּ, וְאֶת יוֹם הַשְּׁבִיעִי מִשֵּׁשֶׁת יְמֵי הַמַּעֲשֶׂה קִדַּשְׁתָּ, הִבְדַּלְתָּ וְקִדַּשְׁתָּ אֶת עַמְּךָ יִשְׂרָאֵל בִּקְדֻשָּׁתֶךָ. בָּרוּךְ אַתָּה יְיָ, הַמַּבְדִּיל בֵּין קֹדֶשׁ לְקֹדֶשׁ:

Böruch atöh adonöy, elohaynu melech hö-olöm, she-heche-yönu v'kiy'mönu v'higi-önu liz'man ha-zeh.

בָּרוּךְ אַתָּה יְיָ אֱלֹהֵינוּ מֶלֶךְ הָעוֹלָם, שֶׁהֶחֱיָנוּ וְקִיְּמָנוּ וְהִגִּיעָנוּ לִזְמַן הַזֶּה:

44

During Sukkot add: בסוכות:

Böruch atöh adonöy elohaynu בָּרוּךְ אַתָּה יְיָ אֱלֹהֵינוּ

melech hö-olöm, asher kid'shönu מֶלֶךְ הָעוֹלָם, אֲשֶׁר קִדְּשָׁנוּ

b'mitzvosöv v'tzivönu בְּמִצְוֹתָיו וְצִוָּנוּ

layshayv ba-suköh. לֵישֵׁב בַּסֻּכָּה:

Blessed are You, Lord our God, King of the universe, Who creates the lights of fire. Blessed are You, Lord our God, King of the universe, Who makes a distinction between sacred and profane, between light and darkness, between Israel and the nations, between the Seventh Day and the six work days; between the holiness of the Shabbat and the holiness of the Festival You have made a distinction, and have sanctified the Seventh Day above the six work days. You have set apart and made holy Your people Israel with Your holiness. Blessed are You Lord, Who makes a distinction between holy and holy. Blessed are you, Lord our God, King of the universe, Who has granted us life, sustained us and enabled us to reach this occasion. On Sukkot: Blessed are You, Lord our God, King of the universe, Who has sanctified us with His commandments, and commanded us to dwell in the Sukkah.

Sit down and drink at least two ounces. Distribute some wine to everyone present. Proceed with the washing of the hands for bread (p. 52).

Kiddush for Rosh Hashana Eve

When Rosh Hashana occurs on a weekday, begin from *Savri Mörönön* (next page). When the Festival occurs on Shabbat, recite quietly from *Shölöm Alaychem* until *Yom Hashishi* (pp. 26-31), then begin below from *Yom Hashishi*, and include all parenthesized words in the blessings. On the second night of Rosh Hashana it is customary to place a new fruit (a species of fruit that you have not eaten this season) on the table prior to Kiddush. This fruit is served right after the Kiddush.

Directions for the Kiddush

The Kiddush is recited standing, while holding a cup of wine or grape juice containing at least 3.5 fluid ounces. Fill the cup and lift it with your right hand then transfer it to the left hand. Now lower it into the cupped palm of your right hand (if you write with your left hand, reverse). Lift the cup at least 10 inches above the table. Recite the passages and blessings below.

On Shabbat:	בשבת:
Yom ha-shishi. Va-y'chulu	יוֹם הַשִּׁשִּׁי: וַיְכֻלּוּ
ha-shöma-yim v'hö-öretz v'chöl	הַשָּׁמַיִם וְהָאָרֶץ וְכָל
tz'vö-öm. Va-y'chal elohim ba-yom	צְבָאָם: וַיְכַל אֱלֹהִים בַּיּוֹם
ha-sh'vi-i, m'lachto asher ösöh,	הַשְּׁבִיעִי, מְלַאכְתּוֹ אֲשֶׁר עָשָׂה,
va-yishbos ba-yom ha-sh'vi-i miköl	וַיִּשְׁבֹּת בַּיּוֹם הַשְּׁבִיעִי מִכָּל
m'lachto asher ösöh. Va-y'vörech	מְלַאכְתּוֹ אֲשֶׁר עָשָׂה: וַיְבָרֶךְ

elohim es yom ha-sh'vi-i,	אֱלֹהִים אֶת יוֹם הַשְּׁבִיעִי,
va-y'kadaysh oso, ki vo shövas	וַיְקַדֵּשׁ אֹתוֹ, כִּי בוֹ שָׁבַת
miköl m'lachto, asher börö	מִכָּל מְלַאכְתּוֹ, אֲשֶׁר בָּרָא
elohim la-asos. **Continue below.**	אֱלֹהִים לַעֲשׂוֹת:

The sixth day. And the heavens and the earth and all their hosts were completed. And God finished by the Seventh Day His work which He had done, and He rested on the Seventh Day from all His work which He had done. And God blessed the Seventh Day and made it holy, for on it He rested from all His work which God created to function.

During the week begin here:

Savri mörönön: Böruch atöh adonöy	סַבְרִי מָרָנָן: בָּרוּךְ אַתָּה יְיָ
elohaynu melech hö-olöm,	אֱלֹהֵינוּ מֶלֶךְ הָעוֹלָם,
boray p'ri ha-göfen.	בּוֹרֵא פְּרִי הַגָּפֶן:

Attention, gentlemen! Blessed are You, Lord our God, King of the universe, Who creates the fruit of the vine.

Böruch atöh adonöy elohaynu	בָּרוּךְ אַתָּה יְיָ אֱלֹהֵינוּ
melech hö-olöm, asher böchar bönu	מֶלֶךְ הָעוֹלָם, אֲשֶׁר בָּחַר בָּנוּ
miköl öm v'ro-m'mönu miköl löshon	מִכָּל עָם וְרוֹמְמָנוּ מִכָּל לָשׁוֹן
v'kid'shönu b'mitzvosöv, va-titen	וְקִדְּשָׁנוּ בְּמִצְוֹתָיו, וַתִּתֶּן
lönu adonöy elohaynu b'ahavöh es	לָנוּ יְיָ אֱלֹהֵינוּ בְּאַהֲבָה אֶת
yom (ha-shabös ha-zeh, v'es yom)	יוֹם (הַשַּׁבָּת הַזֶּה וְאֶת יוֹם)
ha-ziköron ha-zeh, es yom tov	הַזִּכָּרוֹן הַזֶּה, אֶת יוֹם טוֹב

47

Kiddush for Rosh Hashana Eve

מִקְרָא קֹדֶשׁ הַזֶּה, יוֹם
(זִכְרוֹן) תְּרוּעָה (בְּאַהֲבָה) מִקְרָא
קֹדֶשׁ זֵכֶר לִיצִיאַת מִצְרָיִם,
כִּי בָנוּ בָחַרְתָּ וְאוֹתָנוּ קִדַּשְׁתָּ
מִכָּל הָעַמִּים, וּדְבָרְךָ
מַלְכֵּנוּ אֱמֶת וְקַיָּם לָעַד.
בָּרוּךְ אַתָּה יְיָ, מֶלֶךְ עַל כָּל
הָאָרֶץ מְקַדֵּשׁ (הַשַּׁבָּת וְ)
יִשְׂרָאֵל וְיוֹם הַזִּכָּרוֹן:

mikrö kodesh ha-zeh, yom
(zichron) t'ru-öh (b'ahavöh) mikrö
kodesh zaycher litzi-as mitzrö-yim,
ki vönu vöchartö v'osönu kidash-tö
miköl hö-amim, ud'vör'chö
malkaynu emes v'ka-yöm lö-ad.
Böruch atöh adonöy, melech al köl
hö-öretz, m'kadaysh (ha-shabös v')
yisrö-ayl v'yom ha-ziköron.

Blessed are You, Lord our God, King of the universe, Who has chosen us from among all nations, raised us above all tongues, and made us holy through His commandments. And You, Lord our God, have given us in love (on Shabbat: this Shabbat day and) this Day of Remembrance, the Festival of holy assembly, a day for (on Shabbat: the remembrance of) sounding of the shofar, (on Shabbat: in love,) a holy assembly, commemorating the Exodus from Egypt. For You have chosen us and sanctified us from among all the nations, and Your word, our King, is true and enduring forever. Blessed are You Lord, King over all the earth, Who sanctifies (on Shabbat: the Shabbat and) Israel and the Day of Remembrance.

On the first night of Rosh Hashana, continue below with the next blessing.

On the second night of Rosh Hashana, glance at the new fruit, and recite the following blessing. (If a new fruit is not available, the blessing is recited nonetheless.) On Saturday night, first recite Havdalah (p. 44)

Kiddush for Rosh Hashana Eve

Böruch atöh adonöy, elohaynu
melech hö-olöm, she-heche-yönu
v'kiy'mönu v'higi-önu
liz'man ha-zeh.

בָּרוּךְ אַתָּה יְיָ אֱלֹהֵינוּ
מֶלֶךְ הָעוֹלָם, שֶׁהֶחֱיָנוּ
וְקִיְּמָנוּ וְהִגִּיעָנוּ
לִזְמַן הַזֶּה:

Blessed are you, Lord our God, King of the universe, Who has granted us life, sustained us and enabled us to reach this occasion.

Sit down and drink at least two ounces. Distribute some wine to everyone.

On the first night of Rosh Hashana

Proceed with the washing of the hands for bread (p. 52). After eating some bread, take a piece of apple and dip it in honey, then recite the blessing below and eat the apple. Proceed with the meal.

On the second night of Rosh Hashana

Make the blessing over fruit (below) and eat the new fruit. Proceed with the washing of the the hands for bread (p. 52) and the meal.

Böruch atöh adonöy, elohaynu
melech hö-olöm, boray p'ri hö-aytz.

בָּרוּךְ אַתָּה יְיָ אֱלֹהֵינוּ
מֶלֶךְ הָעוֹלָם, בּוֹרֵא פְּרִי הָעֵץ:

On the first night of Rosh Hashanah add:

Y'hi rötzon mil'fönechö
shet'chadaysh ölaynu
shönöh tovöh um'suköh.

יְהִי רָצוֹן מִלְפָנֶיךָ
שֶׁתְּחַדֵּשׁ עָלֵינוּ
שָׁנָה טוֹבָה וּמְתוּקָה:

Blessed are you, Lord our God, King of the universe, Who creates the fruit of the tree. May it be Your will to renew for us a good and sweet year.

49

Kiddush for Festivals & Rosh Hashana Day

On Pesach, Shavuot, and Sukkot begin here.
On Rosh Hashana, begin with *Tik'u* (on the following page).

Askinu s'udösö d'malkö	אַתְקִינוּ סְעוּדָתָא דְמַלְכָּא
sh'laymösö chedvösö d'malkö	שְׁלֵימָתָא חֶדְוָתָא דְמַלְכָּא
ka-dishö dö hi s'udösö d'kud-shö	קַדִּישָׁא דָא הִיא סְעוּדָתָא דְקוּדְשָׁא
b'rich hu ush'chintayh.	בְּרִיךְ הוּא וּשְׁכִינְתֵּיהּ :

Prepare the meal of the King, the complete delight of the Holy King. This is the meal of the Holy One, blessed be He, and His Shechinah. (ed.: Kabbalistic term for a manifestation of God's presence).

Directions for the Kiddush

The Kiddush is recited standing, while holding a cup of wine or grape juice containing at least 3.5 fluid ounces. Fill the cup and lift it with your right hand then transfer it to the left hand. Now lower it into the cupped palm of your right hand (if you write with your left hand, reverse). Lift the cup at least 10 inches above the table. Recite the passages and blessings below.

On Pesach, Shavuot and Sukkot:	לשלש רגלים :
Ay-leh mo-aday adonöy mikrö-ay	אֵלֶּה מוֹעֲדֵי יְיָ מִקְרָאֵי
kodesh asher tik-r'u osöm	קֹדֶשׁ אֲשֶׁר תִּקְרְאוּ אֹתָם
b'mo-adöm. **Continue below.**	בְּמוֹעֲדָם :

These are the Festivals of the Lord, holy assemblies, which you shall proclaim at their appointed times.

Kiddush for Festivals & Rosh Hashana Day

On Rosh Hashana: לראש השנה:

תִּקְעוּ בַחְדֶשׁ שׁוֹפָר, בַּכֶּסֶה
לְיוֹם חַגֵּנוּ. כִּי חֹק לְיִשְׂרָאֵל
הוּא, מִשְׁפָּט לֵאלֹהֵי יַעֲקֹב:

Tik'u va-chodesh shoför, ba-keseh
l'yom cha-gaynu. Ki chok l'yisrö-ayl
hu, mishpöt lay-lohay ya-akov.

Blow the shofar on the New Moon, on the designated day of our Holy Day.
For it is a decree for Israel, a [day of] judgment for the God of Jacob.

Continue below:

סַבְרִי מָרָנָן: בָּרוּךְ אַתָּה יְיָ
אֱלֹהֵינוּ מֶלֶךְ הָעוֹלָם,
בּוֹרֵא פְּרִי הַגָּפֶן:

Savri mörönön: Böruch atöh adonöy
elohaynu melech hö-olöm,
boray p'ri ha-göfen.

Attention, gentlemen! Blessed are You, Lord our God, King of the universe,
Who creates the fruit of the vine.

During Sukkot add: בסוכות:

בָּרוּךְ אַתָּה יְיָ אֱלֹהֵינוּ
מֶלֶךְ הָעוֹלָם, אֲשֶׁר קִדְּשָׁנוּ
בְּמִצְוֹתָיו וְצִוָּנוּ
לֵישֵׁב בַּסֻּכָּה:

Böruch atöh adonöy elohaynu
melech hö-olöm, asher kid'shönu
b'mitzvosöv v'tzivönu
layshayv ba-suköh.

Blessed are You, Lord our God, King of the universe, Who has sanctified us
with His commandments, and commanded us to dwell in the Sukkah.

Sit down and drink at least two ounces. Distribute some wine to everyone
present. Proceed with the washing of the hands for bread (p. 52).

Washing the Hands for Bread

Remove any rings. Fill a large cup with at least 3.5 ounces of cold water, while holding it in your right hand. Transfer the cup to your left hand and pour three times over your whole right hand. Transfer it to your right hand and pour three times over your whole left hand. Rub your hands together and recite the blessing below:

Böruch atöh adonöy elohaynu   בָּרוּךְ אַתָּה יְיָ, אֱלֹהֵינוּ

melech hö-olöm, asher kid'shönu   מֶלֶךְ הָעוֹלָם, אֲשֶׁר קִדְּשָׁנוּ

b'mitzvosöv, v'tzivönu   בְּמִצְוֹתָיו, וְצִוָּנוּ

al n'tilas yödö-yim.   עַל נְטִילַת יָדָיִם:

Blessed are You, Lord our God, King of the universe, Who has sanctified us with His commandments, and commanded us concerning the washing of the hands.

Dry your hands. Return to your seat and do not talk until you have made the blessing over and have eaten a piece of *Challah* or bread. Uncover the two *Challot*. Hold both *Challot* side by side. Graze the knife over a nice, well-baked part of the right Challah. Recite the following blessing:

Böruch atöh adonöy   בָּרוּךְ אַתָּה יְיָ,

elohaynu melech hö-olöm,   אֱלֹהֵינוּ מֶלֶךְ הָעוֹלָם,

hamo-tzi lechem min hö-öretz.   הַמּוֹצִיא לֶחֶם מִן הָאָרֶץ:

Blessed are You, Lord our God, King of the universe, Who brings forth bread from the earth.

Cut a piece, dip it three times in salt* and take a bite. Pass slices around to the assembled family and guests. Now enjoy your meal!

*From Rosh Hashana until the last two days of Sukkot it is customary to substitute honey for salt. This expresses our wish for a sweet new year.

A Meaningful Shabbat & Yom Tov Meal

In addition to the delicious food and drinks that are part of a traditional festive meal, a truly inspired Shabbat and Yom Tov meal is one that is infused with words of Torah, stories with Jewish values, and plenty of Jewish songs and melodies. It is those interactions that bind the physical with the spiritual, inspiring spiritual growth and creating an everlasting impact.

Thankfully, Jewish bookstores today are replete with books that are easy to read and understand on the weekly Torah portion, age-old and new stories, inspirational table readings, and many similar items. A visit (after Shabbat and Yom Tov of course) will most certainly help you create a great Shabbat and Holiday atmosphere for yourself, your family, and for all of your guests.

Grace After Meals

Following the meal we offer thanks to God for the nourishment He has provided us. The prefatory psalms below set the tone for the grace to follow.

On Shabbat or Festivals, begin on page 56. On weekdays, begin below.

On weekdays begin here:
Al na-haros bövel shöm yö-shavnu
gam bö-chinu b'zöch'raynu es
tziyon. Al arövim b'sochöh
tölinu kinoro-saynu. Ki shöm
sh'aylunu sho-vaynu div'ray shir
v'solö-laynu sim-chöh shiru lönu
mishir tziyon. Aych nöshir es shir
adonöy al ad'mas nay-chör. Im
eshkö-chaych y'rushölö-yim
tish-kach y'mini. Tidbak l'shoni
l'chiki im lo ez-k'raychi im
lo a-aleh es y'rushöla-yim al
rosh sim-chösi. Z'chor adonöy
liv'nay edom ays yom
y'rushölö-yim hö-om'rim öru öru
ad ha-y'sod böh. Bas bövel

לְחוֹל :
עַל נַהֲרוֹת בָּבֶל שָׁם יָשַׁבְנוּ
גַּם בָּכִינוּ בְּזָכְרֵנוּ אֶת
צִיּוֹן : עַל עֲרָבִים בְּתוֹכָהּ
תָּלִינוּ כִּנֹּרוֹתֵינוּ : כִּי שָׁם
שְׁאֵלוּנוּ שׁוֹבֵינוּ דִּבְרֵי שִׁיר
וְתוֹלָלֵינוּ שִׂמְחָה שִׁירוּ לָנוּ
מִשִּׁיר צִיּוֹן : אֵיךְ נָשִׁיר אֶת שִׁיר
יְיָ עַל אַדְמַת נֵכָר : אִם
אֶשְׁכָּחֵךְ יְרוּשָׁלָיִם
תִּשְׁכַּח יְמִינִי : תִּדְבַּק לְשׁוֹנִי
לְחִכִּי אִם לֹא אֶזְכְּרֵכִי אִם
לֹא אַעֲלֶה אֶת יְרוּשָׁלַיִם עַל
רֹאשׁ שִׂמְחָתִי : זְכֹר יְיָ
לִבְנֵי אֱדוֹם אֵת יוֹם
יְרוּשָׁלָיִם הָאֹמְרִים עָרוּ עָרוּ
עַד הַיְסוֹד בָּהּ : בַּת בָּבֶל

ha-sh'dudöh ashray she-y'shalem הַשְּׁדוּדָה אַשְׁרֵי שֶׁיְשַׁלֶּם
löch es g'mulaych she-gömalt לָךְ אֶת גְּמוּלֵךְ שֶׁגָּמַלְתְּ
lönu. Ashray she-yochayz v'nipaytz לָנוּ: אַשְׁרֵי שֶׁיֹּאחֵז וְנִפֵּץ
es olö-la-yich el ha-söla. אֶת עֹלָלַיִךְ אֶל הַסָּלַע:

By the rivers of Babylon, there we sat and wept as we remembered Zion. There, upon the willows we hung our harps. For there our captors demanded of us songs, and those Who scorned us — rejoicing, [saying,] "Sing to us the songs of Zion." How can we sing the song of the Lord on alien soil? If I forget you, Jerusalem, let my right hand forget its dexterity. Let my tongue cleave to my palate if I will not remember you, if I will not bring to mind Jerusalem during my greatest joy! Remember, O Lord, against the Edomites the day of the destruction of Jerusalem, when they said, "Raze it, raze it to its very foundation!" O Babylon, who are destined to be laid waste, happy is he who will repay you in retribution for what you have inflicted on us. Happy is he who will seize and crush your infants against the rock!

Lam'na-tzay-ach bin'ginos לַמְנַצֵּחַ בִּנְגִינֹת
mizmor shir. Elohim y'chönaynu מִזְמוֹר שִׁיר: אֱלֹהִים יְחָנֵּנוּ
vivö-r'chaynu, yö-ayr pönöv itönu וִיבָרְכֵנוּ, יָאֵר פָּנָיו אִתָּנוּ
selöh. Löda-as bö-öretz סֶלָה: לָדַעַת בָּאָרֶץ
darkechö, b'chöl go-yim דַּרְכֶּךָ, בְּכָל גּוֹיִם
y'shu-ösechö. Yo-duchö amim יְשׁוּעָתֶךָ: יוֹדוּךָ עַמִּים
elohim, yo-duchö amim kulöm. אֱלֹהִים, יוֹדוּךָ עַמִּים כֻּלָּם:
Yis-m'chu vira-n'nu l'umim, ki יִשְׂמְחוּ וִירַנְּנוּ לְאֻמִּים, כִּי

55

sishpot amim mishor, ul'umim
bö-öretz tan-chaym selöh. Yo-duchö
amim elohim, yo-duchö amim
kulöm. Eretz nös'nöh y'vulöh,
y'vö-r'chaynu elohim elohaynu.
Y'vö-r'chaynu elohim, v'yir'u oso
köl af'say öretz. **Continue with** *Avorchöh.*

תִּשְׁפֹּט עַמִּים מִישׁר, וּלְאֻמִּים
בָּאָרֶץ תַּנְחֵם סֶלָה : יוֹדוּךְ
עַמִּים אֱלֹהִים, יוֹדוּךָ עַמִּים
כֻּלָּם. אֶרֶץ נָתְנָה יְבוּלָהּ,
יְבָרְכֵנוּ אֱלֹהִים אֱלֹהֵינוּ :
יְבָרְכֵנוּ אֱלֹהִים, וְיִירְאוּ אֹתוֹ
כָּל אַפְסֵי אָרֶץ : אברכה

For the Choirmaster; a song with instrumental music; a Psalm. May God be gracious to us and bless us, may He make His countenance shine upon us forever; that Your way be known on earth, Your salvation among all nations. The nations will extol You, O God; all the nations will extol You. The nations will rejoice and sing for joy, for You will judge the peoples justly and guide the nations on earth forever. The peoples will extol You, O God; all the peoples will extol You, for the earth will have yielded its produce and God, our God, will bless us. God will bless us; and all, from the furthest corners of the earth, shall fear Him.

On Shabbat and Festivals begin here:

Shir ha-ma-alos b'shuv adonöy es
shivas tzi-yon hö-yinu k'chol'mim.
Öz yi-mölay s'chok pinu
ul'shonaynu rinöh öz yom'ru
vago-yim higdil adonöy la-asos im
ay-leh. Higdil adonöy la-asos

שִׁיר הַמַּעֲלוֹת בְּשׁוּב יְיָ אֶת
שִׁיבַת צִיּוֹן הָיִינוּ כְּחֹלְמִים :
אָז יִמָּלֵא שְׂחוֹק פִּינוּ
וּלְשׁוֹנֵנוּ רִנָּה אָז יֹאמְרוּ
בַגּוֹיִם הִגְדִּיל יְיָ לַעֲשׂוֹת עִם
אֵלֶּה : הִגְדִּיל יְיָ לַעֲשׂוֹת

imönu hö-yinu s'maychim.	עִמָּנוּ הָיִינוּ שְׂמֵחִים :
Shuvöh adonöy es sh'visaynu	שׁוּבָה יְיָ אֶת שְׁבִיתֵנוּ
ka-afikim ba-negev. Ha-zor'im	כַּאֲפִיקִים בַּנֶּגֶב : הַזֹּרְעִים
b'dim-öh b'rinöh yik-tzoru.	בְּדִמְעָה בְּרִנָּה יִקְצֹרוּ :
Höloch yay-laych uvöcho	הָלוֹךְ יֵלֵךְ וּבָכֹה
nosay meshech ha-zöra bo yövo	נֹשֵׂא מֶשֶׁךְ הַזָּרַע בֹּא יָבֹא
v'rinöh nosay alumosöv.	בְרִנָּה נֹשֵׂא אֲלֻמֹּתָיו :

A song of Ascents. When the Lord will return the exiles of Zion, we will have been like dreamers. Then our mouth will be filled with laughter, and our tongue with songs of joy; then will they say among the nations, "The Lord has done great things for these." The Lord has done great things for us; we were joyful. Lord, return our exiles as streams to arid soil. Those who sow in tears will reap with songs of joy. He goes along weeping, carrying the bag of seed; he will surely return with songs of joy, carrying his sheaves.

Liv'nay korach mizmor shir	לִבְנֵי קֹרַח מִזְמוֹר שִׁיר
y'sudöso b'har'ray kodesh. Ohayv	יְסוּדָתוֹ בְּהַרְרֵי קֹדֶשׁ : אֹהֵב
adonöy sha-aray tziyon mikol	יְיָ שַׁעֲרֵי צִיּוֹן מִכֹּל
mish-k'nos ya-akov. Nich-bödos	מִשְׁכְּנוֹת יַעֲקֹב : נִכְבָּדוֹת
m'dubör böch ir hö-elohim selöh.	מְדֻבָּר בָּךְ עִיר הָאֱלֹהִים סֶלָה :
Azkir rahav uvövel l'yo-d'öy	אַזְכִּיר רַהַב וּבָבֶל לְיֹדְעָי
hinay f'leshes v'tzor im kush zeh	הִנֵּה פְלֶשֶׁת וְצוֹר עִם כּוּשׁ זֶה
yulad shöm. Ul'tziyon yay-ömar ish	יֻלַּד שָׁם : וּלְצִיּוֹן יֵאָמַר אִישׁ
v'ish yulad böh v'hu y'cho-n'nehö	וְאִישׁ יֻלַּד בָּהּ וְהוּא יְכוֹנְנֶהָ

57

elyon. Adonöy yispor bich'sov	עֶלְיוֹן : יְיָ יִסְפֹּר בִּכְתוֹב
amim zeh yulad shöm selöh.	עַמִּים זֶה יֻלַּד שָׁם סֶלָה :
V'shörim k'cho-l'lim kol	וְשָׁרִים כְּחֹלְלִים כֹּל
ma-yönai böch.	מַעְיָנַי בָּךְ :

By the sons of Korach, a Psalm, a Song Whose basic theme is the holy mountains [of Zion and Jerusalem]. The Lord loves the gates of Zion more than all the dwelling places of Jacob. Glorious things are spoken of you, eternal city of God. I will remind Rahav and Babylon concerning my beloved; Philistia and Tyre as well as Ethiopia, "This one was born there." And to Zion will be said, "This person and that was born there"; and He, the Most High, will establish it. The Lord will count in the register of people, "This one was born there." Selah. Singers as well as dancers [will sing your praise and say], "All my inner thoughts are of you."

Avö-r'chöh es adonöy b'chöl ays	אֲבָרְכָה אֶת יְיָ בְּכָל עֵת
tömid t'hilöso b'fi. Sof dövör	תָּמִיד תְּהִלָּתוֹ בְּפִי : סוֹף דָּבָר
ha-kol nishmö es hö-elohim y'rö	הַכֹּל נִשְׁמָע אֶת הָאֱלֹהִים יְרָא
v'es mitzvosöv sh'mor ki zeh köl	וְאֶת מִצְוֹתָיו שְׁמוֹר כִּי זֶה כָּל
hö-ödöm. T'hilas adonöy y'daber pi,	הָאָדָם : תְּהִלַּת יְיָ יְדַבֶּר פִּי
vivö-raych kol bösör shaym köd-sho	וִיבָרֵךְ כָּל בָּשָׂר שֵׁם קָדְשׁוֹ
l'olöm vö-ed. Va-anachnu n'vöraych	לְעוֹלָם וָעֶד : וַאֲנַחְנוּ נְבָרֵךְ
yöh may-atöh v'ad olöm hal'luyöh.	יָהּ מֵעַתָּה וְעַד עוֹלָם הַלְלוּיָהּ :

I will bless the Lord at all times; His praise is always in my mouth. Ultimately, all is known: Fear God, and observe His commandments; for this is the whole purpose of man. My mouth will utter the praise of the Lord; let all flesh bless His holy Name forever. And we will bless the Lord from now to eternity. Praise the Lord.

Grace After Meals

"Mayim Acharonim" - Washing the Fingertips

Prepare a small cup with water. Pour a little water over the fingertips of both hands into a bowl. Bring your fingertips over your lips (except on Passover). Remove the bowl with the water from the table.

Before washing the fingertips, say: קודם מים אחרונים יאמר:

Zeh chaylek ödöm röshö זֶה חֵלֶק אָדָם רָשָׁע

may-elohim v'nachalas מֵאֱלֹהִים וְנַחֲלַת

imro may-ayl. אִמְרוֹ מֵאֵל:

After washing the fingertips, say: אחר מים אחרונים יאמר:

Va-y'dabayr aylai zeh ha-shulchön וַיְדַבֵּר אֵלַי זֶה הַשֻּׁלְחָן

asher lif'nay adonöy. אֲשֶׁר לִפְנֵי יְיָ:

This is the portion of a wicked man from God, and the heritage assigned to him by God. And he said to me: This is the table that is before the Lord.

On Shabbat, Festivals, and Weekdays

When at least three men are saying Grace together, one person leads the Grace and begins with the short "Call to Grace" found below. Otherwise, proceed directly with the Grace on page 61.

In the Presence of a Groom and Bride (during the first 7 days)

Special blessing called "*Sheva Brochos*" are recited after concluding the Grace After Meals. Fill two cups of wine. The leader takes one cup in his right hand and recites the "Call to Grace," remembering to include the appropriate substitutions for a Wedding Feast, and leads the Grace. The other cup is used afterward for the Sheva Brochos.

Grace After Meals

The leader begins:	אם מברכים בזימון אומר המברך :
Rabo-sai mir vel'n ben-tsh'n.	רַבּוֹתַי מִיר וֶועלִין בֶּעְנְטְשִׁין :
The others answer:	ועונין המסובין :
Y'hi shaym adonöy m'voröch	יְהִי שֵׁם יְיָ מְבֹרָךְ
may-atöh v'ad olöm.	מֵעַתָּה וְעַד עוֹלָם :
The leader continues:	המברך אומר :
Y'hi shaym adonöy m'voröch	יְהִי שֵׁם יְיָ מְבֹרָךְ
may-atöh v'ad olöm.	מֵעַתָּה וְעַד עוֹלָם :
Bir'shus mö-rönön	בִּרְשׁוּת מָרָנָן
v'ra-bönön v'ra-bosai n'vö-raych...	וְרַבָּנָן וְרַבּוֹתַי נְבָרֵךְ
With 10 men add: Elohaynu...	(ואם הם עשרה : ... אֱלֹהֵינוּ...)
Otherwise continue:	שֶׁאָכַלְנוּ מִשֶּׁלּוֹ :
...she-öchalnu mi-shelo.	ועונין המסובין ,
The others answer, followed by the leader:	ואחריהם המברך :
Böruch (elohaynu) she-öchalnu	בָּרוּךְ (אֱלֹהֵינוּ)
mi-shelo uv'tuvo chö-yinu.	שֶׁאָכַלְנוּ מִשֶּׁלּוֹ וּבְטוּבוֹ חָיִינוּ :

At a wedding feast, the leader substitutes:	בסעודת נשואין אומר המברך :
N'vöraych elohaynu sheha-simchöh	נְבָרֵךְ אֱלֹהֵינוּ שֶׁהַשִּׂמְחָה
bim'ono she-öchalnu mi-shelo.	בִּמְעוֹנוֹ שֶׁאָכַלְנוּ מִשֶּׁלּוֹ :
The others answer, followed by the leader:	ועונין המסובין , ואחריהם המברך :
Böruch elohaynu sheha-simchöh bim'ono	בָּרוּךְ אֱלֹהֵינוּ שֶׁהַשִּׂמְחָה בִּמְעוֹנוֹ
she-öchalnu mi-shelo uv'tuvo chö-yinu.	שֶׁאָכַלְנוּ מִשֶּׁלּוֹ וּבְטוּבוֹ חָיִינוּ :

Gentlemen, let us say the blessings. May the name of the Lord be blessed from now and to all eternity. With your permission, esteemed gentlemen, let us bless

Grace After Meals

Him (If at least ten men are present: our God,) of whose bounty we have eaten.
Blessed be He (If at least ten men are present: our God,) of whose bounty we
have eaten and by whose goodness we live. At a wedding feast: Let us bless our
God in Whose abode there is joy, of Whose bounty we have eaten. Blessed be
our God in Whose abode there is joy, of Whose bounty we have eaten and by
Whose goodness we live.

Böruch atöh adonöy elohaynu
melech hö-olöm, ha-zön es hö-olöm
kulo b'tuvo b'chayn b'chesed
uv'rachamim hu nosayn lechem
l'chöl bösör, ki l'olöm chasdo.
Uv'tuvo ha- gödol imönu tömid lo
chösayr lönu v'al yech-sar lönu
mözon l'olöm vö-ed. Ba-avur sh'mo
ha- gödol ki hu ayl zön um'farnays
lakol umaytiv lakol umay-chin
mözon l'chöl b'riyosöv asher börö
kö-ömur po-say-ach es yödechö
umasbi-a l'chöl chai rötzon.
Böruch atöh adonöy,
ha-zön es ha-kol.

בָּרוּךְ אַתָּה יְיָ אֱלֹהֵינוּ
מֶלֶךְ הָעוֹלָם, הַזָּן אֶת הָעוֹלָם
כֻּלּוֹ בְּטוּבוֹ בְּחֵן בְּחֶסֶד
וּבְרַחֲמִים הוּא נוֹתֵן לֶחֶם
לְכָל בָּשָׂר כִּי לְעוֹלָם חַסְדּוֹ:
וּבְטוּבוֹ הַגָּדוֹל עִמָּנוּ תָּמִיד לֹא
חָסֵר לָנוּ וְאַל יֶחְסַר לָנוּ
מָזוֹן לְעוֹלָם וָעֶד: בַּעֲבוּר שְׁמוֹ
הַגָּדוֹל כִּי הוּא אֵל זָן וּמְפַרְנֵס
לַכֹּל וּמֵטִיב לַכֹּל וּמֵכִין
מָזוֹן לְכָל בְּרִיוֹתָיו אֲשֶׁר בָּרָא
כָּאָמוּר פּוֹתֵחַ אֶת יָדֶךְ
וּמַשְׂבִּיעַ לְכָל חַי רָצוֹן:
בָּרוּךְ אַתָּה יְיָ,
הַזָּן אֶת הַכֹּל:

Blessed are You, Lord our God, King of the universe, Who, in His goodness,
provides sustenance for the entire world with grace, with kindness and with
mercy. He gives food to all flesh, for His kindness is everlasting. Through
His great goodness to us continuously we do not lack [food], and may we

never lack food, for the sake of His great Name. For He, benevolent God, provides nourishment and sustenance for all, does good to all, and prepares food for all His creatures whom He has created, as it is said: You open Your hand and satisfy the desire of every living thing. Blessed are You Lord, Who provides food for all.

No-deh l'chö adonöy elohaynu al
shehin-chaltö la-avosaynu eretz
chemdöh tovöh ur'chövöh v'al
she-ho-tzay-sönu adonöy elohaynu
may-eretz mitzra-yim uf'disönu
mibays avödim v'al
b'ris'chö she-chösamtö biv'söraynu
v'al torös'chö she-limad-tönu
v'al chukechö she-hoda-tönu
v'al cha-yim chayn vö-chesed
she-chonantönu v'al achilas mözon
shö-atöh zön um'farnays osönu
tömid b'chöl yom uv'chöl
ays uv'chöl shö-öh.

נוֹדֶה לְּךָ יְיָ אֱלֹהֵינוּ עַל
שֶׁהִנְחַלְתָּ לַאֲבוֹתֵינוּ אֶרֶץ
חֶמְדָּה טוֹבָה וּרְחָבָה וְעַל
שֶׁהוֹצֵאתָנוּ יְיָ אֱלֹהֵינוּ
מֵאֶרֶץ מִצְרַיִם וּפְדִיתָנוּ
מִבֵּית עֲבָדִים וְעַל
בְּרִיתְךָ שֶׁחָתַמְתָּ בִּבְשָׂרֵנוּ
וְעַל תּוֹרָתְךָ שֶׁלִּמַּדְתָּנוּ
וְעַל חֻקֶּיךָ שֶׁהוֹדַעְתָּנוּ
וְעַל חַיִּים חֵן וָחֶסֶד
שֶׁחוֹנַנְתָּנוּ וְעַל אֲכִילַת מָזוֹן
שָׁאַתָּה זָן וּמְפַרְנֵס אוֹתָנוּ
תָּמִיד בְּכָל יוֹם וּבְכָל
עֵת וּבְכָל שָׁעָה :

We offer thanks to You, Lord our God, for having given as a heritage to our ancestors a precious, good and spacious land; for having brought us out, Lord our God, from the land of Egypt and redeemed us from the house of bondage; for Your covenant which You have sealed in our flesh; for Your Torah which You have taught us; for Your statutes which You have made known to us; for the life, favor and kindness which You have graciously

Grace After Meals

bestowed upon us; and for the food we eat with which You constantly nourish and sustain us every day, at all times, and at every hour.

On Shabbat or weekdays, continue on page 66.
On Chanukah and Purim, add the portions below.

On Chanukah and Purim: לחנוכה ופורים:

V'al ha-nisim v'al ha-purkön	וְעַל הַנִּסִּים וְעַל הַפֻּרְקָן
v'al ha-g'vuros v'al ha-t'shu-os	וְעַל הַגְּבוּרוֹת וְעַל הַתְּשׁוּעוֹת
v'al ha-niflö-os she-ösisö	וְעַל הַנִּפְלָאוֹת שֶׁעָשִׂיתָ
la-avosaynu ba-yömim hö-haym	לַאֲבוֹתֵינוּ בַּיָּמִים הָהֵם
biz'man ha-zeh.	בִּזְמַן הַזֶּה:

And [we thank You] for the miracles, for the redemption, for the mighty deeds, for the saving acts, and for the wonders which You have wrought for our ancestors in those days, at this time.

On Chanukah: לחנוכה:

Bi-may matis-yöhu ben yochö-nön	בִּימֵי מַתִּתְיָהוּ בֶּן יוֹחָנָן
kohayn gödol chash-monö-i	כֹּהֵן גָּדוֹל, חַשְׁמוֹנַאִי
uvönöv, k'she-öm'döh mal'chus	וּבָנָיו, כְּשֶׁעָמְדָה מַלְכוּת
yövön hö-r'shö-öh al	יָוָן הָרְשָׁעָה, עַל
am'chö yisrö-ayl, l'hashki-chöm	עַמְּךָ יִשְׂרָאֵל, לְהַשְׁכִּיחָם
torö-sechö ul'ha-aviröm	תּוֹרָתֶךָ וּלְהַעֲבִירָם
may-chukay r'tzonechö, v'atöh	מֵחֻקֵּי רְצוֹנֶךָ, וְאַתָּה
b'ra-chamechö hö-rabim ömad-tö	בְּרַחֲמֶיךָ הָרַבִּים עָמַדְתָּ
löhem b'ays tzörösöm. Ravtö es	לָהֶם בְּעֵת צָרָתָם. רַבְתָּ אֶת

63

rivöm, dantö es dinöm, nökamtö es
nik'mösöm. Mösartö giborim b'yad
chalöshim, v'rabim b'yad m'atim,
ut'may-im b'yad t'horim, ur'shö-im
b'yad tzadikim, v'zaydim b'yad
os'kay sorö-sechö. Ul'chö ösisö
shaym gödol v'ködosh
bö-olömechö, ul'am'chö yisrö-ayl
ösisö t'shu-öh g'dolöh ufurkön
k'ha-yom ha-zeh. V'achar kach bö-u
vö-nechö lid'vir bay-sechö, ufinu es
hay-chölechö, v'tiharu es
mikdöshechö v'hid-liku nayros
b'chat'zros köd-shechö, v'köv'u
sh'monas y'may chanuköh aylu
l'hodos ul'halayl l'shim'chö hagödol.

רִיבָם, דַּנְתָּ אֶת דִּינָם, נָקַמְתָּ אֶת
נִקְמָתָם. מָסַרְתָּ גִבּוֹרִים בְּיַד
חַלָּשִׁים, וְרַבִּים בְּיַד מְעַטִּים,
וּטְמֵאִים בְּיַד טְהוֹרִים, וּרְשָׁעִים
בְּיַד צַדִּיקִים, וְזֵדִים בְּיַד
עוֹסְקֵי תוֹרָתֶךָ. וּלְךָ עָשִׂיתָ
שֵׁם גָּדוֹל וְקָדוֹשׁ
בְּעוֹלָמֶךָ, וּלְעַמְּךָ יִשְׂרָאֵל
עָשִׂיתָ תְּשׁוּעָה גְדוֹלָה וּפֻרְקָן
כְּהַיּוֹם הַזֶּה. וְאַחַר כַּךְ בָּאוּ
בָנֶיךָ לִדְבִיר בֵּיתֶךָ, וּפִנּוּ אֶת
הֵיכָלֶךָ, וְטִהֲרוּ אֶת
מִקְדָּשֶׁךָ, וְהִדְלִיקוּ נֵרוֹת
בְּחַצְרוֹת קָדְשֶׁךָ, וְקָבְעוּ
שְׁמוֹנַת יְמֵי חֲנֻכָּה אֵלּוּ
לְהוֹדוֹת וּלְהַלֵּל לְשִׁמְךָ הַגָּדוֹל:

In the days of Matisyohu, the son of Yochonon the High Priest, the Hasmonean and his sons, when the wicked Hellenic government rose up against Your people Israel to make them forget Your Torah and violate the decrees of Your will. But You, in Your abounding mercies, stood by them in the time of their distress. You waged their battles, defended their rights and avenged the wrong done to them. You delivered the mighty into the hands of the weak, the many into the hands of the few, the impure into the hands of the pure, the wicked into the hands of the righteous, and the wanton sinners into the hands of those who occupy themselves with Your Torah.

You made a great and holy name for Yourself in Your world, and effected a great deliverance and redemption for Your people to this very day. Then Your children entered the shrine of Your House, cleansed Your Temple, purified Your Sanctuary, kindled lights in Your holy courtyards, and instituted these eight days of Chanukah to give thanks and praise to Your great Name.

On Purim:	לפורים:
Bi-may mör-d'chai v'estayr	בִּימֵי מָרְדְּכַי וְאֶסְתֵּר
b'shushan ha-biröh, k'she-ömad	בְּשׁוּשַׁן הַבִּירָה, כְּשֶׁעָמַד
alay-hem hömön hö-röshö, bikaysh	עֲלֵיהֶם הָמָן הָרָשָׁע, בִּקֵּשׁ
l'hashmid la-harog ul'abayd es köl	לְהַשְׁמִיד לַהֲרֹג וּלְאַבֵּד אֶת כָּל
ha-y'hudim mi-na-ar v'ad zökayn	הַיְּהוּדִים מִנַּעַר וְעַד זָקֵן
taf v'nöshim b'yom echöd	טַף וְנָשִׁים בְּיוֹם אֶחָד
bish'loshöh ösör l'chodesh sh'naym	בִּשְׁלֹשָׁה עָשָׂר לְחֹדֶשׁ שְׁנֵים
ösör hu chodesh adör ush'lölöm	עָשָׂר הוּא חֹדֶשׁ אֲדָר וּשְׁלָלָם
lövoz, v'atöh b'rachamechö hö-rabim	לָבוֹז, וְאַתָּה בְּרַחֲמֶיךָ הָרַבִּים
hay-fartö es atzöso, v'kil-kaltö es	הֵפַרְתָּ אֶת עֲצָתוֹ, וְקִלְקַלְתָּ אֶת
ma-chashavto, va-hashay-vosö lo	מַחֲשַׁבְתּוֹ, וַהֲשֵׁבוֹתָ לּוֹ
g'mulo b'rosho v'sölu oso	גְּמוּלוֹ בְּרֹאשׁוֹ, וְתָלוּ אוֹתוֹ
v'es bönöv al hö-aytz.	וְאֶת בָּנָיו עַל הָעֵץ:

In the days of Mordechai and Esther, in Shushan the capital, when the wicked Haman rose up against them, and sought to destroy, slaughter and annihilate all the Jews, young and old, infants and women, in one day, on the thirteenth day of the twelfth month, the month of Adar, and to take their spoil for plunder. But You, in Your abounding mercies, foiled his counsel *and frustrated his intention, and caused the evil he planned to recoil on his own head, and they hanged him and his sons upon the gallows.*

All continue below:

V'al ha-kol adonöy elohaynu	וְעַל הַכֹּל יְיָ אֱלֹהֵינוּ
anachnu modim löch um'vö-r'chim	אֲנַחְנוּ מוֹדִים לָךְ וּמְבָרְכִים
osöch yis-böraych shim'chö b'fi köl	אוֹתָךְ יִתְבָּרֵךְ שִׁמְךָ בְּפִי כָּל
chai tömid l'olöm vö-ed. Ka-kösuv	חַי תָּמִיד לְעוֹלָם וָעֶד : כַּכָּתוּב
v'öchaltö v'sövö-tö uvay-rachtö es	וְאָכַלְתָּ וְשָׂבָעְתָּ וּבֵרַכְתָּ אֶת
adonöy elohechö al hö-öretz	יְיָ אֱלֹהֶיךָ עַל הָאָרֶץ
ha-tovöh asher nösan löch.	הַטֹּבָה אֲשֶׁר נָתַן לָךְ :
Böruch atöh adonöy,	בָּרוּךְ אַתָּה יְיָ,
al hö-öretz v'al ha-mözon.	עַל הָאָרֶץ וְעַל הַמָּזוֹן :

For all this, Lord our God, we give thanks to You and bless You. May Your Name be blessed by the mouth of every living being, constantly and forever. As it is written: When you have eaten and are satiated, you shall bless the Lord your God for the good land which He has given you. Blessed are You Lord, for the land and for the sustenance.

Ra-chaym adonöy elohaynu	רַחֵם יְיָ אֱלֹהֵינוּ
al yisrö-ayl amechö v'al	עַל יִשְׂרָאֵל עַמֶּךָ וְעַל
y'rushöla-yim i-rechö v'al tziyon	יְרוּשָׁלַיִם עִירֶךָ וְעַל צִיּוֹן
mishkan k'vodechö v'al mal'chus	מִשְׁכַּן כְּבוֹדֶךָ וְעַל מַלְכוּת
bays dövid m'shichechö v'al	בֵּית דָּוִד מְשִׁיחֶךָ וְעַל
ha-ba-yis ha-gödol v'ha-ködosh	הַבַּיִת הַגָּדוֹל וְהַקָּדוֹשׁ

she-nikrö shim'chö ölöv. Elohaynu	שֶׁנִּקְרָא שְׁמְךָ עָלָיו: אֱלֹהֵינוּ
övinu ro-aynu **(on weekdays: r'aynu)**	אָבִינוּ רוֹעֵנוּ (בחול: רְעֵנוּ)
zonaynu par-n'saynu v'chal-k'laynu	זוֹנֵנוּ פַּרְנְסֵנוּ וְכַלְכְּלֵנוּ
v'harvi-chaynu v'harvach lönu	וְהַרְוִיחֵנוּ וְהַרְוַח לָנוּ
adonöy elohaynu m'hayröh miköl	יְיָ אֱלֹהֵינוּ מְהֵרָה מִכָּל
tzöro-saynu. V'nö al tatzri-chaynu	צָרוֹתֵינוּ: וְנָא אַל תַּצְרִיכֵנוּ
adonöy elohaynu, lo liday mat'nas	יְיָ אֱלֹהֵינוּ, לֹא לִידֵי מַתְּנַת
bösör vödöm v'lo liday	בָּשָׂר וָדָם וְלֹא לִידֵי
halvö-ösöm ki im l'yöd'chö	הַלְוָאָתָם כִּי אִם לְיָדְךָ
ha-m'lay-öh ha-p'suchöh	הַמְּלֵאָה הַפְּתוּחָה
ha-k'doshöh v'hö-r'chövöh shelo	הַקְּדוֹשָׁה וְהָרְחָבָה שֶׁלֹּא
nay-vosh v'lo nikö-laym	נֵבוֹשׁ וְלֹא נִכָּלֵם
l'olöm vö-ed.	לְעוֹלָם וָעֶד:

Have mercy, Lord our God, upon Israel Your people, upon Jerusalem Your city, upon Zion the abode of Your glory, upon the kingship of the house of David Your anointed, and upon the great and holy House over which Your Name was proclaimed. Our God, our Father, Our Shepherd (On weekdays substitute: tend us), nourish us, sustain us, feed us and provide us with plenty, and speedily, Lord our God, grant us relief from all our afflictions. Lord our God, please do not make us dependent upon the gifts of mortal men nor upon their loans, but only upon Your full, open, holy and generous hand, that we may never be shamed or disgraced.

Grace After Meals

On Shabbat: בשבת:

R'tzay v'hachali-tzaynu adonöy
elohaynu b'mitzvo-sechö uv'mitzvas
yom ha-sh'vi-i ha-shabös ha-gödol
v'ha-ködosh ha-zeh ki yom zeh
gödol v'ködosh hu l'fönechö,
lishbös bo v'lönu-ach bo b'ahavöh
k'mitzvas r'tzonechö, uvir'tzon'chö
hö-ni-ach lönu adonöy elohaynu
shelo s'hay tzöröh v'yögon
va-anöchöh b'yom m'nuchö-saynu,
v'har-aynu adonöy elohaynu
b'nechömas tziyon i-rechö
uv'vinyan y'rushöla-yim ir
köd-shechö ki atöh hu ba'al
ha-y'shu-os uva-al ha-nechömos.

רְצֵה וְהַחֲלִיצֵנוּ יְיָ
אֱלֹהֵינוּ בְּמִצְוֹתֶיךָ וּבְמִצְוַת
יוֹם הַשְּׁבִיעִי הַשַּׁבָּת הַגָּדוֹל
וְהַקָּדוֹשׁ הַזֶּה כִּי יוֹם זֶה
גָּדוֹל וְקָדוֹשׁ הוּא לְפָנֶיךָ,
לִשְׁבָּת בּוֹ וְלָנוּחַ בּוֹ בְּאַהֲבָה
כְּמִצְוַת רְצוֹנֶךָ, וּבִרְצוֹנְךָ
הָנִיחַ לָנוּ יְיָ אֱלֹהֵינוּ
שֶׁלֹּא תְהֵא צָרָה וְיָגוֹן
וַאֲנָחָה בְּיוֹם מְנוּחָתֵנוּ,
וְהַרְאֵנוּ יְיָ אֱלֹהֵינוּ
בְּנֶחָמַת צִיּוֹן עִירֶךָ,
וּבְבִנְיַן יְרוּשָׁלַיִם עִיר
קָדְשֶׁךָ כִּי אַתָּה הוּא בַּעַל
הַיְשׁוּעוֹת וּבַעַל הַנֶּחָמוֹת:

May it please You, Lord our God, to strengthen us through Your mitzvot, and through the mitzvah of the Seventh Day, this great and holy Shabbat. For this day is great and holy before You, to refrain from work and to rest thereon with love, in accordance with the commandment of Your will. In Your good will, Lord our God, bestow upon us tranquility, that there shall be no distress, sadness or sorrow on the day of our rest. Lord our God, let us see the consolation of Zion Your city, and the rebuilding of Jerusalem Your holy city, for You are the Master of deliverance and the Master of consolation.

On Rosh Chodesh and Festivals:

בר"ח וביו"ט ובחוה"מ:

Elohaynu vaylo-hay avosaynu	אֱלֹהֵינוּ וֵאלֹהֵי אֲבוֹתֵינוּ
ya-aleh v'yövo, v'yagi-a v'yayrö-eh	יַעֲלֶה וְיָבֹא, וְיַגִּיעַ וְיֵרָאֶה
v'yayrö-tzeh, v'yishöma v'yipökayd	וְיֵרָצֶה, וְיִשָּׁמַע וְיִפָּקֵד
v'yizöchayr, zichro-naynu	וְיִזָּכֵר, זִכְרוֹנֵנוּ
ufik'do-naynu, v'zichron	וּפִקְדוֹנֵנוּ, וְזִכְרוֹן
avosaynu, v'zichron möshi-ach	אֲבוֹתֵינוּ, וְזִכְרוֹן מָשִׁיחַ
ben dövid av-dechö, v'zichron	בֶּן דָּוִד עַבְדֶּךָ, וְזִכְרוֹן
y'rushöla-yim ir köd-shechö,	יְרוּשָׁלַיִם עִיר קָדְשֶׁךָ,
v'zichron köl am'chö bays yisrö-ayl	וְזִכְרוֹן כָּל עַמְּךָ בֵּית יִשְׂרָאֵל
l'fönechö lif'laytöh l'tovöh, l'chayn	לְפָנֶיךָ לִפְלֵיטָה לְטוֹבָה, לְחֵן
ul'chesed ul'rachamim ul'cha-yim	וּלְחֶסֶד וּלְרַחֲמִים וּלְחַיִּים
tovim ul'shölom b'yom...	טוֹבִים וּלְשָׁלוֹם, בְּיוֹם...

On Rosh Chodesh:	בר"ח:
rosh ha-chodesh ha-zeh.	רֹאשׁ הַחֹדֶשׁ הַזֶּה.
On Pesach:	בפסח:
chag ha-matzos ha-zeh.	חַג הַמַּצּוֹת הַזֶּה.
On Shavuot:	בשבועות:
chag ha-shövu-os ha-zeh.	חַג הַשָּׁבֻעוֹת הַזֶּה.
On Sukkot:	בסוכות:
chag ha-sukos ha-zeh.	חַג הַסֻּכּוֹת הַזֶּה.
On Shmini Atzeret and Simchat Torah:	בשמ"ע ושמח"ת:
sh'mini atzeres ha-chag ha-zeh.	שְׁמִינִי עֲצֶרֶת הַחַג הַזֶּה.

On Rosh Hashana: בר"ה:

ha-ziköron ha-zeh. הַזִּכָּרוֹן הַזֶּה.

On Pesach, Shavuot, Sukkot (except on Chol בשלש רגלים
HaMoed), and Rosh Hashana: (חוץ מחוה"מ) ובר"ה:

b'yom tov mikrö kodesh ha-zeh. בְּיוֹם טוֹב מִקְרָא קֹדֶשׁ הַזֶּה.

Zöch'raynu adonöy elohaynu bo זָכְרֵנוּ יְיָ אֱלֹהֵינוּ בּוֹ

l'tovöh, ufök'daynu vo liv'röchöh, לְטוֹבָה, וּפָקְדֵנוּ בּוֹ לִבְרָכָה,

v'hoshi-aynu vo l'cha-yim tovim. וְהוֹשִׁיעֵנוּ בּוֹ לְחַיִּים טוֹבִים:

Uvid'var y'shu-öh v'rachamim וּבִדְבַר יְשׁוּעָה וְרַחֲמִים

chus v'chönaynu v'rachaym ölaynu חוּס וְחָנֵּנוּ וְרַחֵם עָלֵינוּ

v'hoshi-aynu ki aylechö aynaynu, וְהוֹשִׁיעֵנוּ כִּי אֵלֶיךָ עֵינֵינוּ,

ki ayl melech chanun כִּי אֵל מֶלֶךְ חַנּוּן

v'rachum ötöh. וְרַחוּם אָתָּה:

Our God and God of our fathers, may there ascend, come and reach, be seen, accepted, and heard, recalled and remembered before You, the remembrance and recollection of us, the remembrance of our fathers, the remembrance of Mashiach the son of David Your servant, the remembrance of Jerusalem Your holy city, and the remembrance of all Your people the House of Israel, for deliverance, well-being, grace, kindness, mercy, good life and peace, on this day of: On Rosh Chodesh: *Rosh Chodesh.* On Pesach: *the Festival of Matzot.* On Shavuot: *the Festival of Shavuot.* On Sukkot: *the Festival of Sukkot.* On Shemini Atzeret and Simchat Torah: *Shemini Atzeret, the Festival.* On Rosh Hashana: *Remembrance.* On Pesach, Shavuot, and Sukkot - except on Chol HaMoed - and on Rosh Hashana: *On this holy Festival day. Remember us on this [day], Lord our God, for good; be mindful of us on this [day] for blessing; help us on this [day] for good life. With the promise of deliverance and compassion, spare us and be gracious to us; have mercy upon us and deliver us; for our eyes are directed to You, for You, God, are a gracious and merciful King.*

All continue below:

Uv'nay y'rushöla-yim ir ha-kodesh	וּבְנֵה יְרוּשָׁלַיִם עִיר הַקֹּדֶשׁ
bim'hayröh v'yömaynu. Böruch	בִּמְהֵרָה בְיָמֵינוּ. בָּרוּךְ
atöh adonöy, bonay v'rachamöv	אַתָּה יְיָ, בֹּנֵה בְרַחֲמָיו
y'rushölö-yim. Ömayn.	יְרוּשָׁלָיִם. אָמֵן.

And rebuild Jerusalem the holy city speedily in our days. Blessed are You Lord, Who in His mercy rebuilds Jerusalem. Amen.

Boruch atöh adonöy elohaynu	בָּרוּךְ אַתָּה יְיָ אֱלֹהֵינוּ
melech hö-olöm, hö-ayl, övinu	מֶלֶךְ הָעוֹלָם, הָאֵל, אָבִינוּ
malkaynu, adi-raynu bor'aynu	מַלְכֵּנוּ, אַדִּירֵנוּ בּוֹרְאֵנוּ
go-alaynu yo-tz'raynu, k'do-shaynu	גּוֹאֲלֵנוּ יוֹצְרֵנוּ, קְדוֹשֵׁנוּ
k'dosh ya-akov, ro-aynu ro-ay	קְדוֹשׁ יַעֲקֹב, רוֹעֵנוּ רוֹעֵה
yisrö-ayl, ha-melech ha-tov	יִשְׂרָאֵל, הַמֶּלֶךְ הַטּוֹב
v'ha-maytiv lakol b'chöl yom	וְהַמֵּטִיב לַכֹּל בְּכָל יוֹם
vö-yom, hu hay-tiv lönu, hu	וָיוֹם, הוּא הֵיטִיב לָנוּ, הוּא
may-tiv lönu, hu yay-tiv lönu,	מֵטִיב לָנוּ, הוּא יֵיטִיב לָנוּ,
hu g'mölönu hu gom'laynu	הוּא גְמָלָנוּ הוּא גוֹמְלֵנוּ
hu yig-m'laynu lö-ad, l'chayn	הוּא יִגְמְלֵנוּ לָעַד, לְחֵן

ul'chesed ul'racha-mim, ul'revach	וּלְחֶסֶד וּלְרַחֲמִים, וּלְרֶוַח
ha-tzölöh v'hatzlöchöh, b'röchöh	הַצָּלָה וְהַצְלָחָה, בְּרָכָה
vishu-öh, nechömöh par-nösöh	וִישׁוּעָה, נֶחָמָה פַּרְנָסָה
v'chal-kölöh v'rachamim v'cha-yim	וְכַלְכָּלָה וְרַחֲמִים וְחַיִּים
v'shölom v'chöl tov, umiköl	וְשָׁלוֹם וְכָל טוֹב, וּמִכָּל
tuv l'olöm al y'chas'raynu.	טוּב לְעוֹלָם אַל יְחַסְּרֵנוּ׃

Blessed are You, Lord our God, King of the universe, benevolent God, our Father, our King, our Strength, our Creator, our Redeemer, our Maker, our Holy One, the Holy One of Jacob, our Shepherd, the Shepherd of Israel, the King Who is good and does good to all, each and every day. He has done good for us, He does good for us, and He will do good for us; He has bestowed, He bestows, and He will forever bestow upon us grace, kindness and mercy, relief, salvation and success, blessing and deliverance, consolation, livelihood and sustenance, compassion, life, peace and all goodness; and may He never cause us to lack any good.

Hörachamön hu yimloch ölaynu	הָרַחֲמָן הוּא יִמְלוֹךְ עָלֵינוּ
l'olöm vö-ed. Hörachamön hu	לְעוֹלָם וָעֶד׃ הָרַחֲמָן הוּא
yisböraych ba-shöma-yim	יִתְבָּרֵךְ בַּשָּׁמַיִם
uvö-öretz. Hörachamön hu	וּבָאָרֶץ׃ הָרַחֲמָן הוּא
yish-tabach l'dor dorim v'yispö-ayr	יִשְׁתַּבַּח לְדוֹר דּוֹרִים וְיִתְפָּאֵר
bönu lö-ad ul'nay-tzach n'tzöchim	בָּנוּ לָעַד וּלְנֵצַח נְצָחִים
v'yis-hadar bönu lö-ad ul'ol'may	וְיִתְהַדַּר בָּנוּ לָעַד וּלְעוֹלְמֵי
olömim. Hörachamön hu	עוֹלָמִים׃ הָרַחֲמָן הוּא

y'far-n'saynu b'chövod. : יְפַרְנְסֵנוּ בְּכָבוֹד

Hörachamön hu yish-bor ol gölus הָרַחֲמָן הוּא יִשְׁבּוֹר עוֹל גָּלוּת

may-al tzavö-raynu v'hu yoli-chaynu מֵעַל צַוָּארֵנוּ וְהוּא יוֹלִיכֵנוּ

kom'miyus l'ar-tzaynu. : קוֹמְמִיּוּת לְאַרְצֵנוּ

Hörachamön hu yishlach b'röchöh הָרַחֲמָן הוּא יִשְׁלַח בְּרָכָה

m'ruböh b'va-yis zeh v'al shulchön מְרֻבָּה בְּבַיִת זֶה וְעַל שֻׁלְחָן

zeh she-öchalnu ölöv. Hörachamön זֶה שֶׁאָכַלְנוּ עָלָיו : הָרַחֲמָן

hu yishlach lönu es ayli-yöhu הוּא יִשְׁלַח לָנוּ אֶת אֵלִיָּהוּ

ha-növi zöchur latov vi-vaser lönu הַנָּבִיא זָכוּר לַטּוֹב וִיבַשֶּׂר לָנוּ

b'soros tovos y'shu-os v'ne-chömos. : בְּשׂוֹרוֹת טוֹבוֹת יְשׁוּעוֹת וְנֶחָמוֹת

Hörachamön hu y'vöraych es övi הָרַחֲמָן הוּא יְבָרֵךְ אֶת אָבִי

mori ba-al haba-yis ha-zeh v'es imi מוֹרִי בַּעַל הַבַּיִת הַזֶּה וְאֶת אִמִּי

morösi ba-las haba-yis ha-zeh מוֹרָתִי בַּעֲלַת הַבַּיִת הַזֶּה

osöm v'es baysöm v'es zar-öm v'es אוֹתָם וְאֶת בֵּיתָם וְאֶת זַרְעָם וְאֶת

köl asher löhem osönu v'es köl כָּל אֲשֶׁר לָהֶם אוֹתָנוּ וְאֶת כָּל

asher lönu. K'mo shebay-rach es אֲשֶׁר לָנוּ : כְּמוֹ שֶׁבֵּרַךְ אֶת

avosaynu avröhöm yitz-chök אֲבוֹתֵינוּ אַבְרָהָם יִצְחָק

v'ya-akov bakol mikol kol kayn וְיַעֲקֹב בַּכֹּל מִכֹּל כֹּל כֵּן

y'vöraych osönu (b'nay v'ris) kulönu יְבָרֵךְ אוֹתָנוּ (בְּנֵי בְרִית) כֻּלָּנוּ

yachad biv'röchöh sh'laymöh יַחַד בִּבְרָכָה שְׁלֵמָה

v'nomar ömayn. : וְנֹאמַר אָמֵן

May the Merciful One reign over us forever and ever. May the Merciful One be blessed in heaven and on earth. May the Merciful One be praised for all generations, and pride Himself in us forever and to all eternity, and glorify

Himself in us forever and ever. May the Merciful One provide our livelihood with honor. May the Merciful One break the yoke of exile from our neck and may He lead us upright to our land. May the Merciful One send abundant blessing into this house and upon this table at which we have eaten. May the Merciful One send us Elijah the prophet — may he be remembered for good — and let him bring us good tidings, deliverance and consolation. May the Merciful One bless my father, my teacher, the master of this house, and my mother, my teacher, the mistress of this house; them, their household, their children, and all that is theirs; us, and all that is ours. Just as He blessed our forefathers, Abraham, Isaac and Jacob, "in all things," "by all things," with "all things," so may He bless all of us together (the children of the Covenant) with a perfect blessing, and let us say, Amen.

Mimörom y'lam'du ölöv v'ölaynu	מִמָּרוֹם יְלַמְּדוּ עָלָיו וְעָלֵינוּ
z'chus shet'hay l'mish-meres	זְכוּת שֶׁתְּהֵא לְמִשְׁמֶרֶת
shölom v'nisö v'röchöh may-ays	שָׁלוֹם וְנִשָּׂא בְרָכָה מֵאֵת
adonöy utz'dököh may-elohay	יְיָ וּצְדָקָה מֵאֱלֹהֵי
yish-aynu v'nimtzö chayn v'saychel	יִשְׁעֵנוּ וְנִמְצָא חֵן וְשֵׂכֶל
tov b'aynay elohim v'ödöm.	טוֹב בְּעֵינֵי אֱלֹהִים וְאָדָם :

From heaven, may there be invoked upon him and upon us such merit which will bring enduring peace. May we receive blessing from the Lord and kindness from God our Deliverer, and may we find grace and good understanding in the eyes of God and man.

Grace After Meals

On Shabbat add: :בשבת

Hörachamön hu yan-chilaynu הָרַחֲמָן הוּא יַנְחִילֵנוּ
l'yom she-kulo shabös um'nuchöh לְיוֹם שֶׁכֻּלּוֹ שַׁבָּת וּמְנוּחָה
l'cha-yay hö-olömim. לְחַיֵּי הָעוֹלָמִים :

May the Merciful One let us inherit that day which will be all Shabbat and rest for life everlasting.

On Rosh Chodesh add: :בר"ח

Hörachamön hu y'chadaysh הָרַחֲמָן הוּא יְחַדֵּשׁ
ölaynu es ha-chodesh ha-zeh עָלֵינוּ אֶת הַחֹדֶשׁ הַזֶּה
l'tovöh v'liv'röchöh. לְטוֹבָה וְלִבְרָכָה :

May the Merciful One renew for us this month for good and for blessing.

On Festivals add: :ביו"ט

Horachamön hu yan-chilaynu הָרַחֲמָן הוּא יַנְחִילֵנוּ
l'yom she-kulo tov. לְיוֹם שֶׁכֻּלּוֹ טוֹב :

May the Merciful One let us inherit that day which is all good.

On Rosh Hashana add: :לר"ה

Hörachamön hu y'chadaysh הָרַחֲמָן הוּא יְחַדֵּשׁ
ölaynu es ha-shönöh ha-zos עָלֵינוּ אֶת הַשָּׁנָה הַזֹּאת
l'tovöh v'liv'röchöh. לְטוֹבָה וְלִבְרָכָה :

May the Merciful One renew for us this year for good and for blessing.

Grace After Meals

On Sukkot add: :בסוכות

Hörachamön hu yökim lönu הָרַחֲמָן הוּא יָקִים לָנוּ
es sukas dövid ha-nofeles. :אֶת סֻכַּת דָּוִד הַנּוֹפֶלֶת

May the Merciful One restore for us the fallen sukkah of David.

All continue below:

Hörachamön hu y'zakaynu liymos הָרַחֲמָן הוּא יְזַכֵּנוּ לִימוֹת
ha-möshi-ach ul'cha-yay hö-olöm הַמָּשִׁיחַ וּלְחַיֵּי הָעוֹלָם
habö. Migdol (On weekdays: Magdil) הַבָּא. מִגְדּוֹל (בחול: מַגְדִּיל)
y'shu-os malko v'oseh יְשׁוּעוֹת מַלְכּוֹ וְעֹשֶׂה
chesed lim'shicho l'dövid ul'zar-o חֶסֶד לִמְשִׁיחוֹ לְדָוִד וּלְזַרְעוֹ
ad olöm. O-seh shölom bim'romöv עַד עוֹלָם: עֹשֶׂה שָׁלוֹם בִּמְרוֹמָיו
hu ya-aseh shölom ölaynu v'al הוּא יַעֲשֶׂה שָׁלוֹם עָלֵינוּ וְעַל
köl yisrö-ayl v'im'ru ömayn. :כָּל יִשְׂרָאֵל וְאִמְרוּ אָמֵן

May the Merciful One grant us the privilege of reaching the days of the Mashiach and the life of the World to Come. He is a tower of deliverance (on Weekdays substitute: He gives great deliverance) to His king, and bestows kindness upon His anointed, to David and his descendants forever. He Who makes peace in His heavens, may He make peace for us and for all Israel; and say, Amen.

Y'ru es adonöy k'doshöv ki ayn יְראוּ אֶת יְיָ קְדֹשָׁיו כִּי אֵין
mach-sor liray-öv. K'firim röshu מַחְסוֹר לִירֵאָיו: כְּפִירִים רָשׁוּ
v'rö-ayvu v'dor'shay adonöy lo וְרָעֵבוּ וְדֹרְשֵׁי יְיָ לֹא
yach-s'ru chöl tov. Hodu la-donöy יַחְסְרוּ כָל טוֹב: הוֹדוּ לַיְיָ
ki tov ki l'olöm chasdo. :כִּי טוֹב כִּי לְעוֹלָם חַסְדּוֹ

76

Po-say-ach es yödechö umas-bi-a פּוֹתֵחַ אֶת יָדֶךָ וּמַשְׂבִּיעַ
l'chöl chai rötzon. Böruch ha-gever לְכָל חַי רָצוֹן: בָּרוּךְ הַגֶּבֶר
asher yiv-tach ba-donöy אֲשֶׁר יִבְטַח בַּיְיָ
v'hö-yöh adonöy miv-tachö. : וְהָיָה יְיָ מִבְטַחוֹ

Fear the Lord, you His holy ones, for those who fear Him suffer no want. Young lions are in need and go hungry, but those who seek the Lord shall not lack any good. Give thanks to the Lord for He is good, for His kindness is everlasting. You open Your hand and satisfy the desire of every living thing. Blessed is the man who trusts in the Lord, and the Lord will be his security.

**"Sheva Brochot" blessings recited at
a wedding feast, are found on page 82.**

Grace After a Snack or Wine

The following is said after eating at least 1 ounce of cooked or baked food prepared from the five species of grain [wheat, barley, rye, oats or spelt], and after eating wine, grapes, figs, pomegranates, olives or dates. If one ate any of these fruits, and also ate cake and/or drank wine (or grape juice), he should combine the items together in the blessing. For other foods and drinks (except bread), recite *Boray N'föshos* (p. 81).

Böruch atöh adonöy elohaynu בָּרוּךְ אַתָּה יְיָ אֱלֹהֵינוּ
melech hö-olöm מֶלֶךְ הָעוֹלָם

Grace After a Snack or Wine

After foods prepared from the five grains:
al ha-mich-yöh v'al ha-kalkölöh...

על ה' מיני דגן :
עַל הַמִּחְיָה וְעַל הַכַּלְכָּלָה...

After wine:
(v')al ha-gefen v'al p'ri ha-gefen...

על היין :
(וְ)עַל הַגֶּפֶן וְעַל פְּרִי הַגֶּפֶן...

After grapes, figs,
pomegranates, olives or dates:
(v')al hö-aytz v'al p'ri hö-aytz...

על פירות
מז' מינים :
(וְ)עַל הָעֵץ וְעַל פְּרִי הָעֵץ...

...v'al t'nuvas ha-sö-deh v'al eretz
chemdöh tovöh ur'chövöh
sherö-tzisö v'hin-chaltö la-avosaynu
le-echol mipir-yöh v'lisbo-a
mi-tuvöh, rachem nö adonöy
elohaynu al yisrö-ayl amechö v'al
y'rushöla-yim irechö v'al tziyon
mishkan k'vodechö v'al
miz-b'chechö v'al hay-chölechö
uv'nay y'rushöla-yim ir ha-kodesh
bim'hayröh v'yömaynu v'ha-alaynu
l'sochöh, v'sam'chaynu vöh
un'vörech'chö bi'kdushö uv'töhöröh,

...וְעַל תְּנוּבַת הַשָּׂדֶה וְעַל אֶרֶץ
חֶמְדָּה טוֹבָה וּרְחָבָה
שֶׁרָצִיתָ וְהִנְחַלְתָּ לַאֲבוֹתֵינוּ
לֶאֱכוֹל מִפִּרְיָהּ וְלִשְׂבּוֹעַ
מִטּוּבָהּ' רַחֶם נָא יְיָ
אֱלֹהֵינוּ עַל יִשְׂרָאֵל עַמֶּךָ וְעַל
יְרוּשָׁלַיִם עִירֶךָ וְעַל צִיּוֹן
מִשְׁכַּן כְּבוֹדֶךָ וְעַל
מִזְבְּחֶךָ וְעַל הֵיכָלֶךָ
וּבְנֵה יְרוּשָׁלַיִם עִיר הַקֹּדֶשׁ
בִּמְהֵרָה בְיָמֵינוּ וְהַעֲלֵנוּ
לְתוֹכָהּ, וְשַׂמְּחֵנוּ בָהּ
וּנְבָרֶכְךָ בִּקְדֻשָּׁה וּבְטָהֳרָה,

Grace After a Snack or Wine

On Shabbat: בשבת:
ur'tzay v'hachali-tzaynu b'yom וּרְצֵה וְהַחֲלִיצֵנוּ בְּיוֹם
ha-shabös ha-zeh. הַשַּׁבָּת הַזֶּה.

On Rosh Chodesh, Festivals, בר״ח ויו״ט
and Chol HaMoed: ובחוה״מ:
v'zöch'raynu l'tovöh b'yom... ...וְזָכְרֵנוּ לְטוֹבָה בְּיוֹם

On Rosh Chodesh: בר״ח:
...rosh ha-chodesh ha-zeh. ...רֹאשׁ הַחֹדֶשׁ הַזֶּה.

On Rosh Hashana: בראש השנה:
...ha-ziköron ha-zeh. ...הַזִּכָּרוֹן הַזֶּה.

On Pesach: בפסח:
...chag ha-matzos ha-zeh. ...חַג הַמַּצּוֹת הַזֶּה.

On Shavuot: בשבועות:
...chag ha-shövu-os ha-zeh. ...חַג הַשָּׁבֻעוֹת הַזֶּה.

On Sukkot: בסוכות:
...chag ha-sukkos ha-zeh. ...חַג הַסֻּכּוֹת הַזֶּה.

On Shmini Atzeret and Simchat Torah: בשמ״ע ושמח״ת:
...sh'mini atzeres ha-chag ha-zeh. ...שְׁמִינִי עֲצֶרֶת הַחַג הַזֶּה.

Ki atöh adonöy tov umaytiv la-kol כִּי אַתָּה יְיָ טוֹב וּמֵטִיב לַכֹּל
v'no-deh l'chö al hö-öretz... ...וְנוֹדֶה לְךָ עַל הָאָרֶץ

After foods prepared from the five grains: על ה׳ מיני דגן:
...v'al ha-mich-yöh. ...וְעַל הַמִּחְיָה.

79

Grace After a Snack or Wine

After wine:	על היין :
...v'al p'ri ha-göfen.	**וְעַל פְּרִי הַגָּפֶן.** ..
After grapes, figs,	על פירות
pomegranates, olives or dates:	מז' מינים :
...v'al ha-payros.	**וְעַל הַפֵּרוֹת.** ..
Böruch atöh adonöy, al hö-öretz...	**בָּרוּךְ אַתָּה יְיָ, עַל הָאָרֶץ** ..
After foods prepared from the five grains:	על ה' מיני דגן :
...v'al ha-mich-yöh.	**וְעַל הַמִּחְיָה** : ..
After wine:	על היין :
...v'al p'ri ha-göfen.	**וְעַל פְּרִי הַגָּפֶן** : ..
After grapes, figs,	על פירות
pomegranates, olives or dates:	מז' מינים :
...v'al ha-payros.	**וְעַל הַפֵּרוֹת** : ..

Blessed are You, Lord our God, King of the universe, for: After prepared foods from the five kinds of grain: *the sustenance and the nourishment,* After wine: *the vine and the fruit of the vine,* After grapes, figs, pomegranates, olives or dates: *the tree and the fruit of the tree ...for the produce of the field, and for the precious, good and spacious land which You have graciously given as a heritage to our ancestors, to eat of its fruit and be satiated with its goodness. Have mercy, Lord our God, on Israel Your people, on Jerusalem Your city, on Zion the abode of Your glory, on Your altar and on Your Temple. Rebuild Jerusalem, the holy city, speedily in our days, and bring us up to it and make us rejoice in it, and we will bless You in holiness and purity. (On Shabbat: May it please You to strengthen us on this Shabbat day.)* On Rosh Chodesh, Festivals and Chol

Grace After a Snack or Wine

HaMoed: *Remember us for good on this day of:* (on Rosh Chodesh: *Rosh Chodesh*). (On Rosh Hashana: *Remembrance*). (On Pesach: the Festival of Matzot). (On Shavuot: *the Festival of Shavuot*). (On Sukkot: *the Festival of Sukkot*). (On Shmini Atzeret and Simchat Torah: *Shmini Atzeret, the Festival*). For You, Lord, are good and do good to all, and we offer thanks to You for the land and for: After food prepared from the five kinds of grain: *the sustenance*. After wine: *(and) the fruit of the vine*. After grapes, figs pomegranates, olives or dates: *(and) the fruits. Blessed are You Lord, for the land.*. After food prepared from the five kinds of grain *...and for the sustenance.* After wine: *and for the fruit of the vine.* After grapes, figs, pomegranates, olives or dates: *and for the fruits.*

Grace After Other Snacks or Drinks

The following blessing is recited after any foods or drink upon which Grace After Meals or Grace After a Snack does not apply (i.e. eggs, cheese, chocolates, candies, ice cream, most drinks (except wine or grape juice)).

Böruch atöh adonöy elohaynu	בָּרוּךְ אַתָּה יְיָ אֱלֹהֵינוּ
melech hö-olöm, boray n'föshos	מֶלֶךְ הָעוֹלָם, בּוֹרֵא נְפָשׁוֹת
rabos v'chesronön al kol mah	רַבּוֹת וְחֶסְרוֹנָן עַל כֹּל מַה
shebörösö l'hacha-yos böhem	שֶׁבָּרֵאתָ לְהַחֲיוֹת בָּהֶם
nefesh köl chöy. Böruch	נֶפֶשׁ כָּל חָי. בָּרוּךְ
chay hö-olömim.	חֵי הָעוֹלָמִים׃

Blessed are You, Lord our God, King of the universe, Creator of numerous living beings and their needs, for all the things You have created with which to sustain the soul of every living being. Blessed is He Who is the Life of the worlds.

"Sheva Brachot"

These blessings are recited following the "Grace After Meals," holding the second cup of wine that was filled prior to reciting the Grace. It is customary to honor different Jewish men with the recitation of each blessing.

1. Böruch atöh adonöy, elohaynu melech hö-olöm, she-hakol börö lich'vodo.

1. בָּרוּךְ אַתָּה יְיָ, אֱלֹהֵינוּ מֶלֶךְ הָעוֹלָם, שֶׁהַכֹּל בָּרָא לִכְבוֹדוֹ:

Blessed are You, Lord our God, King of the universe, Who has created all things for His glory.

2. Böruch atöh adonöy, elohaynu melech hö-olöm, yo-tzayr hö-ödöm.

2. בָּרוּךְ אַתָּה יְיָ, אֱלֹהֵינוּ מֶלֶךְ הָעוֹלָם, יוֹצֵר הָאָדָם:

Blessed are You, Lord our God, King of the universe, Creator of man.

3. Böruch atöh adonöy, elohaynu melech hö-olöm, asher yö-tzar es hö-ödöm b'tzalmo b'tzelem d'mus tavniso, v'hiskin lo mi-menu binyan aday ad. Böruch atöh adonöy, yo-tzayr hö-ödöm.

3. בָּרוּךְ אַתָּה יְיָ, אֱלֹהֵינוּ מֶלֶךְ הָעוֹלָם, אֲשֶׁר יָצַר אֶת הָאָדָם בְּצַלְמוֹ בְּצֶלֶם דְּמוּת תַּבְנִיתוֹ, וְהִתְקִין לוֹ מִמֶּנּוּ בִּנְיַן עֲדֵי עַד: בָּרוּךְ אַתָּה יְיָ, יוֹצֵר הָאָדָם:

Blessed are You, Lord our God, King of the universe, Who created man in His image, in the image [of His] likeness [He fashioned] his form, and prepared for him from His own self an everlasting edifice. Blessed are You Lord, Creator of man.

82

4. Sos tösis v'sögayl hö-aköröh
b'kibutz bö-nehö l'sochöh
b'simchöh. Böruch atöh adonöy,
m'samay-ach tziyon b'vönehö.

4. שׁוֹשׂ תָּשִׂישׂ וְתָגֵל הָעֲקָרָה
בְּקִבּוּץ בָּנֶיהָ לְתוֹכָהּ
בְּשִׂמְחָה: בָּרוּךְ אַתָּה יְיָ,
מְשַׂמֵּחַ צִיּוֹן בְּבָנֶיהָ:

May the barren one [Jerusalem] rejoice and be happy at the ingathering of her children to her midst in joy. Blessed are You Lord, Who gladdens Zion with her children.

5. Samach t'samach ray-im
hö-ahuvim k'samay-chachö
y'tzir'chö b'gan ayden mi-kedem.
Böruch atöh adonöy,
m'samay-ach chösön v'chalöh.

5. שַׂמַּח תְּשַׂמַּח רֵעִים
הָאֲהוּבִים כְּשַׂמֵּחֲךָ
יְצִירְךָ בְּגַן עֵדֶן מִקֶּדֶם:
בָּרוּךְ אַתָּה יְיָ,
מְשַׂמֵּחַ חָתָן וְכַלָּה:

Grant abundant joy to these loving friends, as You bestowed gladness upon Your created being in the Garden of Eden of old. Blessed are You Lord, Who gladdens the groom and bride.

6. Böruch atöh adonöy elohaynu
melech hö-olöm, asher börö söson
v'simchöh chösön v'chalöh, gilöh
ri-nöh di-tzöh v'chedvöh, ahavöh
v'achavöh shölom v'ray-us.
M'hayröh adonöy elohaynu
yi-shöma b'öray y'hudöh,
uv'chu-tzos y'rushölö-yim, kol söson
v'kol simchöh, kol chösön v'kol

6. בָּרוּךְ אַתָּה יְיָ, אֱלֹהֵינוּ
מֶלֶךְ הָעוֹלָם, אֲשֶׁר בָּרָא שָׂשׂוֹן
וְשִׂמְחָה חָתָן וְכַלָּה, גִּילָה
רִנָּה דִּיצָה וְחֶדְוָה, אַהֲבָה
וְאַחֲוָה שָׁלוֹם וְרֵעוּת.
מְהֵרָה יְיָ אֱלֹהֵינוּ
יִשָּׁמַע בְּעָרֵי יְהוּדָה,
וּבְחוּצוֹת יְרוּשָׁלַיִם, קוֹל שָׂשׂוֹן
וְקוֹל שִׂמְחָה, קוֹל חָתָן וְקוֹל

כַּלָּה, קוֹל מִצְהֲלוֹת חֲתָנִים
kalöh, kol mitz-halos cha-sönim
מֵחֻפָּתָם, וּנְעָרִים מִמִּשְׁתֵּה
may-chupösöm un'örim mi-mishtay
נְגִינָתָם: בָּרוּךְ אַתָּה יְיָ,
n'ginösöm. Böruch atöh adonöy,
מְשַׂמֵּחַ חָתָן עִם הַכַּלָּה:
m'samay-ach chösön im ha-kalöh.

Blessed are You, Lord our God, King of the universe, Who created joy and happiness, groom and bride, gladness, jubilation, cheer and delight, love, friendship, harmony and fellowship. Lord our God, let there speedily be heard in the cities of Judah and in the streets of Jerusalem the sound of joy and the sound of happiness, the sound of a groom and the sound of a bride, the sound of exultation of grooms from under their Chupah, and youths from their joyous banquets. Blessed are You Lord, Who gladdens the groom with the bride.

The leader of the Grace takes the cup over which the "Grace After Meals" was recited and recites the following blessing, after which he drinks at least most of the cup.

The leader of the Grace recites: :המברך

7. בָּרוּךְ אַתָּה יְיָ אֱלֹהֵינוּ
7. Böruch atöh adonöy elohaynu
מֶלֶךְ הָעוֹלָם, בּוֹרֵא פְּרִי הַגָּפֶן:
melech hö-olöm, boray p'ri ha-göfen.

Blessed are You, Lord our God, King of the universe, Who creates the fruit of the vine.

The remaining wine is mixed with the wine over which the Sheva Brachot was recited. The groom then drinks some, followed by the bride. The leader of the Grace then recites the Grace After a Snack (for wine) on page 77.

84

Order of The Third Shabbat Meal

The third Shabbat meal is eaten anytime between a half hour after midday and sunset. One should eat bread at this meal (see Washing the Hands for Bread, p. 52). During the meal the following Psalm and hymn are recited:

Mizmor l'dövid, adonöy ro-i lo ech-sör. Bin'os deshe yarbi-tzayni, al may m'nuchos y'nahalayni. Nafshi y'shovayv, yan-chayni v'ma-g'lay tzedek l'ma-an sh'mo. Gam ki ay-laych b'gay tzal-möves lo irö rö, ki atöh imödi, shiv-t'chö umish-antechö hay-möh y'na-chamuni. Ta-aroch l'fönai shulchön neged tzo-r'röy, dishan-tö va-shemen roshi, kosi r'vö-yöh. Ach tov vöchesed yir-d'funi köl y'may cha-yöy, v'shavti b'vays adonöy l'orech yömim.	מִזְמוֹר לְדָוִד, יְיָ רֹעִי לֹא אֶחְסָר : בִּנְאוֹת דֶּשֶׁא יַרְבִּיצֵנִי, עַל מֵי מְנוּחוֹת יְנַהֲלֵנִי : נַפְשִׁי יְשׁוֹבֵב, יַנְחֵנִי בְמַעְגְּלֵי צֶדֶק לְמַעַן שְׁמוֹ : גַּם כִּי אֵלֵךְ בְּגֵיא צַלְמָוֶת לֹא אִירָא רָע, כִּי אַתָּה עִמָּדִי, שִׁבְטְךָ וּמִשְׁעַנְתֶּךָ הֵמָּה יְנַחֲמֻנִי : תַּעֲרֹךְ לְפָנַי שֻׁלְחָן נֶגֶד צֹרְרָי, דִּשַּׁנְתָּ בַשֶּׁמֶן רֹאשִׁי, כּוֹסִי רְוָיָה : אַךְ טוֹב וָחֶסֶד יִרְדְּפוּנִי כָּל יְמֵי חַיָּי, וְשַׁבְתִּי בְּבֵית יְיָ לְאֹרֶךְ יָמִים :

A Psalm by David. The Lord is my shepherd; I shall lack nothing. He makes me lie down in green pastures; He leads me beside still waters. He revives my soul; He directs me in the paths of righteousness for the sake of His

Name. Even if I walk in the valley of the shadow of death, I will fear no evil, for You are with me; Your rod and Your staff – they will comfort me. You will prepare a table before my enemies; You have anointed my head with oil; my cup is full. Only goodness and kindness shall follow me all the days of my life, and I shall dwell in the House of the Lord for many long years.

Askinu s'udösö dim'hay-m'nusö	אַתְקִינוּ סְעוּדָתָא דִמְהֵימְנוּתָא
sh'laymösö chedvösö d'malkö	שְׁלֵמָתָא חֶדְוָתָא דְמַלְכָּא
ka-dishö, askinu s'udösö d'malkö,	קַדִּישָׁא, אַתְקִינוּ סְעוּדָתָא דְמַלְכָּא,
dö hi s'udösö diz'ayr anpin,	דָּא הִיא סְעוּדָתָא דִזְעֵר אַנְפִּין,
v'atikö ka-dishö va-chakal ta-puchin	וְעַתִּיקָא קַדִּישָׁא וַחֲקַל תַּפּוּחִין
ka-dishin, asyön l'sa-adö ba-hadayh.	קַדִּישִׁין, אַתְיָן לְסַעֲדָא בַּהֲדֵיהּ׃

Prepare the meal of perfect faith, which is the delight of the holy King; prepare the meal of the King. This is the meal of "Z'eir Anpin," and the holy Ancient One and the holy "Chakal Tapuchin" (ed.: Kabbalistic terms for manifestations of God's presence) come to join him in the meal.

B'nay hay-chölö, dich'sifin,	בְּנֵי הֵיכָלָא, דִכְסִיפִין,
l'meche-zay ziv diz'ayr an-pin.	לְמֶחֱזֵי זִיו דִזְעֵיר אַנְפִּין׃
Y'hon höchö, b'hai takö, d'vayh	יְהוֹן הָכָא, בְּהַאי תַּכָּא, דְּבֵיהּ
mal-kö b'gilufin. Tz'vu la-chadö,	מַלְכָּא בְּגִלוּפִין׃ צְבוּ לַחֲדָא,
b'hai va-adö, b'go irin v'chöl	בְּהַאי וַעֲדָא, בְּגוֹ עִירִין וְכָל
gad'fin. Chadu hash-tö, b'hai	גַּדְּפִין׃ חֲדוּ הַשְׁתָּא, בְּהַאי
sha-tö, d'vayh ra-avö v'lays za-afin.	שַׁעְתָּא, דְּבֵיהּ רַעֲוָא וְלֵית זַעֲפִין׃

K'rivu li, chazu chay-li, d'lays dinin דis'kifin. L'var nat'lin, v'lö ölin, ha-nay kal-bin dacha-tzifin. V'hö azmin, atik yo-min, l'mitz-chö aday y'hon chal'fin. R'u dilayh, d'galay layh, l'vatölö b'chöl k'lifin. Y'shavay lon b'nok'vay-hon, vi-tam'run b'go chay-fin. Aray ha-shtö, b'minchösö, b'chedvösö diz'ayr anpin.

קְרִיבוּ לִי, חֲזוּ חֵילִי, דְּלֵית דִּינִין
דִּתְקִיפִין: לְבַר נַטְלִין, וְלָא עָאלִין,
הַנֵּי כַּלְבִּין דַּחֲצִיפִין: וְהָא
אַזְמִין, עַתִּיק יוֹמִין, לְמִצְחָא עֲדֵי
יְהוֹן חַלְפִין: רְעוּ דִילֵיהּ, דְּגַלֵּי
לֵיהּ, לְבַטָּלָא בְּכָל קְלִיפִין: יְשַׁוֵּי
לוֹן בְּנוֹקְבֵיהוֹן, וִיטַמְּרוּן בְּגוֹ
כֵּיפִין: אֲרֵי הַשְׁתָּא, בְּמִנְחָתָא,
בְּחֶדְוָתָא דִזְעֵיר אַנְפִּין:

You princes of the palace, Who yearn to behold the splendor of Z'eir Anpin. Be present at this meal at which the King leaves His imprint. Exult, rejoice in this gathering together with the angels and all supernal beings; Rejoice now, at this most propitious time, when there is no sadness. Draw near to Me, behold My strength, for there are no harsh judgments. They are cast out, they may not enter, these [forces of evil which are likened to insolent dogs. I herewith invite the "Ancient of Days" at this auspicious time, and [the powers of impurity] will be utterly removed. It is His revealed will to annul all the powers of impurity; He will hurl them into their abysses, and they will hide in the clefts of the rocks. For this time of Minchah is a time of joy for Z'eir Anpin.

The Havdalah

The Havdalah is recited after nightfall on Saturday, when at least three stars are visible in the sky. It is recited standing, with a cup of wine or grape juice. The cup should contain at least 3.5 ounces. We use sweet aromatic spices and a multi-wick candle as well.

Hold the cup in the palm of your right hand and recite the following:

Hinay, ayl y'shu-ösi ev-tach, v'lo ef-chöd, ki özi v'zimrös yöh adonöy, va-y'hi li lishu-öh. Ush'avtem ma-yim b'söson mi-ma-a-y'nay ha-y'shu-öh. La-donöy ha-y'shu-öh, al am'chö vir'chösechö selöh. Adonöy tz'vö-os i-mönu misgöv lönu elohay ya-akov selöh. Adonöy tz'vö-os ashray ödöm botay-ach böch. Adonöy hoshi-öh, ha-melech ya-anaynu v'yom kör'aynu. La-y'hudim hö-y'söh o-röh v'simchöh, v'söson vikör. Kayn tih-yeh lönu. Kos y'shu-os esö uv'shaym adonöy ekrö.

הִנֵּה, אֵל יְשׁוּעָתִי אֶבְטַח וְלֹא אֶפְחָד, כִּי עָזִּי וְזִמְרָת יָהּ יְיָ, וַיְהִי לִי לִישׁוּעָה: וּשְׁאַבְתֶּם מַיִם בְּשָׂשׂוֹן מִמַּעַיְנֵי הַיְשׁוּעָה: לַיְיָ הַיְשׁוּעָה, עַל עַמְּךָ בִרְכָתֶךָ סֶּלָה: יְיָ צְבָאוֹת עִמָּנוּ מִשְׂגָּב לָנוּ אֱלֹהֵי יַעֲקֹב סֶלָה: יְיָ צְבָאוֹת אַשְׁרֵי אָדָם בֹּטֵחַ בָּךְ: יְיָ הוֹשִׁיעָה, הַמֶּלֶךְ יַעֲנֵנוּ בְיוֹם קָרְאֵנוּ: לַיְּהוּדִים הָיְתָה אוֹרָה וְשִׂמְחָה, וְשָׂשׂוֹן וִיקָר: כֵּן תִּהְיֶה לָּנוּ: כּוֹס יְשׁוּעוֹת אֶשָּׂא וּבְשֵׁם יְיָ אֶקְרָא:

88

The Havdalah

Indeed, God is my deliverance; I am confident and shall not fear, for God the Lord is my strength and song, and He has been a help to me. You shall draw water with joy from the wellsprings of deliverance. Deliverance is the Lord's; may Your blessing be upon Your people forever. The Lord of hosts is with us, the God of Jacob is our everlasting stronghold. Lord of hosts, happy is the man who trusts in You. Lord, help us; may the King answer us on the day we call. For the Jews there was light and joy, gladness and honor — so let it be with us. I raise the cup of deliverance and invoke the Name of the Lord.

Savri mörönön: Böruch atöh adonöy סַבְרִי מָרָנָן : בָּרוּךְ אַתָּה יְיָ
elohaynu melech hö-olöm, אֱלֹהֵינוּ מֶלֶךְ הָעוֹלָם,
boray p'ri ha-göfen. בּוֹרֵא פְּרִי הַגָּפֶן :

Attention, gentlemen! Blessed are You, Lord our God, King of the universe, Who creates the fruit of the vine.

Set the cup down, and recite the following blessing over the spices:

Böruch atöh adonöy elohaynu בָּרוּךְ אַתָּה יְיָ אֱלֹהֵינוּ
melech hö-olöm, boray מֶלֶךְ הָעוֹלָם, בּוֹרֵא
minay v'sömim. מִינֵי בְשָׂמִים :

Blessed are You, Lord our God, King of the universe, Who creates various kinds of spices.

Smell the fragrant spices, then recite the following blessing over the fire:

Böruch atöh adonöy elohaynu בָּרוּךְ אַתָּה יְיָ אֱלֹהֵינוּ
melech hö-olöm, boray מֶלֶךְ הָעוֹלָם, בּוֹרֵא
m'oray hö-aysh. מְאוֹרֵי הָאֵשׁ :

Blessed are You, Lord our God, King of the universe, Who creates the lights of fire.

The Havdalah

Fold the fingers of your hands over the thumb and look at the fingernails using the light of the flame. Turn your palms over in the direction of the flame. Now take the cup with your right hand, give it to your left hand and lower it into your cupped right hand, and recite the following:

Böruch atöh adonöy elohaynu
melech hö-olöm, hamavdil bayn
kodesh l'chol, bayn or l'choshech,
bayn yisrö-ayl lö-amim, bayn yom
hash'vi-i l'shayshes y'may
hama-aseh. Böruch atöh adonöy,
hamavdil bayn kodesh l'chol.

בָּרוּךְ אַתָּה יְיָ אֱלֹהֵינוּ
מֶלֶךְ הָעוֹלָם, הַמַּבְדִּיל בֵּין
קֹדֶשׁ לְחוֹל, בֵּין אוֹר לְחשֶׁךְ,
בֵּין יִשְׂרָאֵל לָעַמִּים, בֵּין יוֹם
הַשְּׁבִיעִי לְשֵׁשֶׁת יְמֵי
הַמַּעֲשֶׂה: בָּרוּךְ אַתָּה יְיָ,
הַמַּבְדִּיל בֵּין קֹדֶשׁ לְחוֹל:

Blessed are You, Lord our God, King of the universe, Who makes a distinction between sacred and profane, between light and darkness, between Israel and the nations, between the Seventh Day and the six work days. Blessed are You Lord, Who makes a distinction between sacred and profane.

On Chol HaMoed Sukkot, in the Sukkah, add: בחוה״מ סוכות:

Böruch atöh adonöy, elohaynu melech
hö-olöm, asher kid'shönu b'mitzvosöv,
v'tzivönu layshayv ba-suköh.

בָּרוּךְ אַתָּה יְיָ, אֱלֹהֵינוּ מֶלֶךְ
הָעוֹלָם, אֲשֶׁר קִדְּשָׁנוּ בְּמִצְוֹתָיו,
וְצִוָּנוּ לֵישֵׁב בַּסֻּכָּה:

Blessed are You, Lord our God, King of the universe, Who has sanctified us with His commandments, and commanded us to dwell in the Sukkah.

Sit down and drink at least 2 ounces from the cup. Pour some of the wine into a dish and put out the flames by dipping the candle(s) into the liquid. Recite the Grace After a Snack (for wine), on page 77.

Popular Shabbat and Festival Table Songs

Shabbat and Festivals bring tremendous joy into the home. The delight of the day is radient, especially while enjoying the festive meals. As singing Jewish songs has always been part of this special experience, we have included a wide range of Jewish songs for everyone. Go around the table and let everyone choose a song!

[Songs are sorted in English alphabetical order]

1. Achas shö-alti may-ays hashem, osöh ava-kaysh, shivti b'vays hashem, köl y'may cha-yai, la-chazos b'no-am hashem, ul'vakayr b'haychölo.

1. אַחַת שָׁאַלְתִּי מֵאֵת ה׳,
אוֹתָהּ אֲבַקֵּשׁ, שִׁבְתִּי בְּבֵית ה׳
כָּל יְמֵי חַיַּי, לַחֲזוֹת בְּנֹעַם
ה׳ וּלְבַקֵּר בְּהֵיכָלוֹ.

One thing I have asked of the Lord, this I seek, that I may dwell in the House of the Lord all the days of my life, to behold the pleasantness of the Lord, and to visit in His Sanctuary.

2. Adon olöm asher mölach, b'terem köl y'tzur nivrö. L'ays na-asöh v'chef-tzo kol, azai melech sh'mo nik-rö. V'acharay kich'los ha-kol, l'vado yimloch norö. V'hu hö-yöh, v'hu ho-veh, v'hu yih-yeh, b'sif-öröh. V'hu echöd v'ayn shayni, l'hamshil lo l'hachbiröh. B'li rayshis b'li sachlis,

2. אֲדוֹן עוֹלָם אֲשֶׁר מָלַךְ, בְּטֶרֶם
כָּל יְצוּר נִבְרָא. לְעֵת נַעֲשָׂה
בְחֶפְצוֹ כֹּל, אֲזַי מֶלֶךְ שְׁמוֹ
נִקְרָא. וְאַחֲרֵי כִּכְלוֹת הַכֹּל,
לְבַדּוֹ יִמְלוֹךְ נוֹרָא. וְהוּא הָיָה,
וְהוּא הֹוֶה, וְהוּא יִהְיֶה, בְּתִפְאָרָה.
וְהוּא אֶחָד וְאֵין שֵׁנִי, לְהַמְשִׁיל לוֹ
לְהַחְבִּירָה. בְּלִי רֵאשִׁית בְּלִי תַכְלִית,

v'lo hö-oz v'hamisröh. V'hu kayli
v'chai go-ali, v'tzur chevli b'ays tzöröh.
V'hu nisi umönos li, m'nös
kosi b'yom ekrö. B'yödo afkid
ruchi, b'ays ishan v'ö-iröh. V'im
ruchi g'vi-yösi, hashem li v'lo irö.

וְלוֹ הָעֹז וְהַמִּשְׂרָה. וְהוּא קֵלִי
וְחַי גֹּאֲלִי, וְצוּר חֶבְלִי בְּעֵת צָרָה.
וְהוּא נִסִּי וּמָנוֹס לִי, מְנָת
כּוֹסִי בְּיוֹם אֶקְרָא. בְּיָדוֹ אַפְקִיד
רוּחִי, בְּעֵת אִישָׁן וְאָעִירָה. וְעִם
רוּחִי גְּוִיָּתִי, ה' לִי וְלֹא אִירָא.

Lord of the universe, Who reigned before anything was created — at the time when by His will all things were made, then was His name proclaimed King. And after all things shall cease to be, the Awesome One will reign alone. He was, He is, and He shall be in glory. He is one, and there is no other to compare to Him, to consort with Him. Without beginning, without end, power and dominion belong to Him. He is my God and my ever-living Redeemer, the strength of my lot in time of distress. He is my banner and my refuge, my portion on the day I call. Into His hand I entrust my spirit, when I sleep and when I awake. And with my soul, my body too, the Lord is with me, I shall not fear.

3. Ayn aroch l'chö v'ayn zulösechö,
efes biltechö, umi do-meh löch.
Ayn aroch l'chö hashem elokaynu
bö-olöm ha-zeh, v'ayn zulös'chö
malkaynu l'cha-yay hö-olöm habö.
Efes bil-t'chö go-alaynu
limos ha-möshi-ach, v'ayn
do-meh l'chö moshi-aynu
lis'chiyas ha-maysim.

3. אֵין עֲרוֹךְ לְךָ וְאֵין זוּלָתֶךָ,
אֶפֶס בִּלְתֶּךָ, וּמִי דוֹמֶה לָּךְ.
אֵין עֲרוֹךְ לְךָ ה' אֱלֹקֵינוּ
בָּעוֹלָם הַזֶּה, וְאֵין זוּלָתְךָ
מַלְכֵּנוּ לְחַיֵּי הָעוֹלָם הַבָּא.
אֶפֶס בִּלְתֶּךָ גּוֹאֲלֵנוּ
לִימוֹת הַמָּשִׁיחַ, וְאֵין
דוֹמֶה לְךָ מוֹשִׁיעֵנוּ
לִתְחִיַּת הַמֵּתִים:

There is none comparable to You, and none apart from You; there is nothing without You, and Who is like You? There is none comparable to You, Lord our God — in this world; and none apart from You, our King — in the life of the World to Come; there is nothing without You, our Redeemer — in the days of Mashiach; and there is none like You, our Deliverer — in the era of the resurrection of the dead.

4. Al hanisim, v'al ha-purkön, v'al ha-g'vuros, v'al ha-t'shu-os, v'al ha-niflö-os, she-ösisö la-avosaynu ba-yömim hö-haym bi'zman ha-zeh.

‏4. עַל הַנִּסִּים, וְעַל הַפֻּרְקָן, וְעַל הַגְּבוּרוֹת, וְעַל הַתְּשׁוּעוֹת, וְעַל הַנִּפְלָאוֹת, שֶׁעָשִׂיתָ לַאֲבוֹתֵינוּ בַּיָּמִים הָהֵם בִּזְמַן הַזֶּה.‏

[We thank You] for the miracles, for the redemption, for the mighty deeds, for the saving acts, and for the wonders which You have wrought for our ancestors in those days, at this time.

5. Al tirö mipachad pis-om umisho-as r'shö-im ki sövo. Utzu ay-tzöh v'suför, dab'ru dövör v'lo yökum, ki imönu kayl.

‏5. אַל תִּירָא מִפַּחַד פִּתְאֹם, וּמִשֹּׁאַת רְשָׁעִים כִּי תָבֹא. עֻצוּ עֵצָה וְתֻפָר, דַּבְּרוּ דָבָר וְלֹא יָקוּם, כִּי עִמָּנוּ קֵל.‏

Do not fear sudden terror, nor the destruction of the wicked when it comes. Contrive a scheme, but it will be foiled; conspire a plot, but it will not materialize, for God is with us.

6. Al ha-sela höch va-yay-tz'u mö-yim.　‏6. עַל הַסֶּלַע הָךְ, וַיֵּצְאוּ מָיִם.‏

He struck the rock and there streamed forth water.

7. Am yisrö-ayl chai. Od övinu chai. ‏7. עַם יִשְׂרָאֵל חַי. עוֹד אָבִינוּ חַי.‏

The people of Israel live. Our Father still lives.

8. Ani ma-amin be-emunöh sh'laymöh b'vi-as hamöshi-ach. V'af al pi she-yismah-may-ah im köl zeh achakeh lo b'chöl yom she-yövo. ‏8. אֲנִי מַאֲמִין בֶּאֱמוּנָה שְׁלֵמָה בְּבִיאַת הַמָּשִׁיחַ, וְאַף עַל פִּי שֶׁיִּתְמַהְמֵהַּ עִם כָּל זֶה אֲחַכֶּה לוֹ בְּכָל יוֹם שֶׁיָּבֹא.‏

I believe with perfect faith in the coming of Moshiach (the Redeemer); and although he may tarry, I will wait daily for his coming.

9. Ani ömarti elokim atem, uv'nay elyon kul'chem. Kumöh elokim shöf'töh hö-öretz, ki atöh sin-chal b'chöl ha-go-yim. ‏9. אֲנִי אָמַרְתִּי אֱלֹקִים אַתֶּם, וּבְנֵי עֶלְיוֹן כֻּלְּכֶם. קוּמָה אֱלֹקִים שָׁפְטָה הָאָרֶץ, כִּי אַתָּה תִנְחַל בְּכָל הַגּוֹיִם.‏

I had said, "You are godlike beings, all of you sons of the most high." Arise, God, judge the earth, for You will inherit all the nations.

10. An-im z'miros v'shirim e-erog, ki aylechö naf-shi sa-arog. Naf-shi chö-m'döh b'tzayl yö-dechö, löda-as köl röz so-dechö. ‏10. אַנְעִים זְמִירוֹת וְשִׁירִים אֶאֱרוֹג, כִּי אֵלֶיךָ נַפְשִׁי תַעֲרוֹג. נַפְשִׁי חָמְדָה בְּצֵל יָדֶךָ, לָדַעַת כָּל רָז סוֹדֶךָ.‏

I shall compose pleasant psalms and weave hymns, because for You shall my soul pine. My soul desired the shelter of your hand, to know every mystery of Your secret.

94

11. Asadayr lis'udösö, b'tzaf-rö d'shabatö, va-azamin böh hashtö, atikö kadishö.

אַסַדֵּר לִסְעוּדָתָא, בְּצַפְרָא .11
דְּשַׁבַּתָּא, וַאֲזַמִּין בָּהּ הַשְׁתָּא,
עַתִּיקָא קַדִּישָׁא :

N'horayh yishray vöh, b'kidushö rabö, uv'chamrö tövö, d'vayh te-che-day nafshö.

נְהוֹרֵיהּ יִשְׁרֵי בָהּ, בְּקִדּוּשָׁא
רַבָּא, וּבְחַמְרָא טָבָא, דְּבֵיהּ
תֶּחֱדֵי נַפְשָׁא :

Y'shadayr lön shufrayh, v'neche-zay viköray, v'ya-chazay lön sisrayh, d'is-amar bil'chishö.

יְשַׁדֵּר לָן שׁוּפְרֵיהּ, וְנֶחֱזֵי
בִיקָרֵיהּ, וְיַחֲזֵי לָן סִתְרֵיהּ,
דְּאִתְאַמַּר בִּלְחִישָׁא :

Y'galay lön ta-amay, d'vis'raysar naha-may, d'inun ös bish'mayh, k'filö uk'lishö.

יְגַלֶּה לָן טַעֲמֵי, דִּבְתְרֵיסַר
נַהֲמֵי, דְּאִנּוּן אָת בִּשְׁמֵיהּ,
כְּפִילָא וּקְלִישָׁא :

Tz'rorö di-l'aylö, d'vay cha-yay cholö, v'yisra-bay chaylö, v'sisak ad rayshö.

צְרוֹרָא דִּלְעֵלָּא, דְּבֵיהּ חַיֵּי כֹלָּא,
וְיִתְרַבֵּי חֵילָא, וְתִסַּק עַד רֵישָׁא :

Chadu chatz-day chaklö, b'dibur uv'kölö, umalilu milöh, m'sikö k'duvshö.

חֲדוּ חַצְדֵּי חַקְלָא, בְּדִבּוּר
וּבְקָלָא, וּמַלִּילוּ מִלָּה,
מְתִיקָא כְּדוּבְשָׁא :

Ködöm ribon öl'min, b'milin s'simin,

קֳדָם רִבּוֹן עָלְמִין, בְּמִלִּין סְתִימִין,

תְּגַלּוּן פִּתְגָּמִין, וְתֵימְרוּן חִדּוּשָׁא: t'galun pisgömin, v'saym'run chidushö.

לְעַטֵּר פָּתוֹרָא, בְּרָזָא יַקִּירָא, עֲמִיקָא וּטְמִירָא, וְלַאו מִלְּתָא אַוְשָׁא: L'atayr p'sorö, b'rözö yakirö, amikö ut'mirö, v'lav mil'sö avshö.

וְאִלֵּין מִלַּיָּא, יְהוֹן לִרְקִיעַיָּא, וְתַמָּן מַאן שַׁרְיָא, הֲלָא הַהוּא שִׁמְשָׁא: V'ilayn mila-yö, y'hon lir'ki-a-yö, v'samön man sharyö, halö ha-hu shim-shö.

רְבוּ יַתִּיר יִסְגֵּי, לְעֵלָּא מִן דַּרְגֵּיהּ, וְיִסַּב בַּת זוּגֵיהּ, דַּהֲוַת פְּרִישָׁא: R'vu yatir yisgay, l'aylö min dar-gayh, v'yisav bas zugayh, dahavas p'rishö.

I shall offer praise at the Shabbat morning meal, and shall herewith invite the holy Ancient One. May the supernal light shine thereon through the great Kiddush and good wine that gladdens the soul. May He send to us its resplendence, and we shall behold its glory; may He reveal to us His hidden things which are said in secret.

12. אֲשֶׁר בָּרָא שָׂשׂוֹן וְשִׂמְחָה חָתָן וְכַלָּה, גִּילָה רִנָּה דִּיצָה וְחֶדְוָה, אַהֲבָה וְאַחֲוָה שָׁלוֹם וְרֵעוּת.   12. Asher börö söson v'simchöh, chösön v'chalöh, gilöh rinöh ditzöh v'chedvöh, ahavöh v'achavöh shölom v'rayus.

[Blessed are You] Who created joy and happiness, groom and bride, gladness, jubilation, cheer and delight, love, friendship, harmony and fellowship.

13. Ashraynu mah tov chel-kaynu,
umah nö-im gorö-laynu,
umah yöföh y'rushö-saynu.

13. אַשְׁרֵינוּ מַה טּוֹב חֶלְקֵנוּ,
וּמַה נָּעִים גּוֹרָלֵנוּ,
וּמַה יָּפָה יְרֻשָּׁתֵנוּ.

Fortunate are we! How good is our portion, how pleasant our lot and how beautiful our heritage!

14. Atöh hö-kayl osay fele hoda-tö
vö-amim uzechö. Gö-altö biz'ro-a
amechö b'nay ya-akov v'yosayf selöh.

14. אַתָּה הָקֵל עֹשֵׂה פֶלֶא הוֹדַעְתָּ
בָעַמִּים עֻזֶּךָ. גָּאַלְתָּ בִזְרוֹעַ
עַמְּךָ בְּנֵי יַעֲקֹב וְיוֹסֵף סֶלָה.

You are the God Who does wonders, You have made known Your strength amongst the nations. You have redeemed Your people with a mighty arm, the children of Yaakov and Yosef.

15. Atöh v'chartönu miköl hö-amim,
öhavtö o-sönu v'rö-tzisö bönu,
v'romam-tönu mi-köl hal'shonos,
v'kidash-tönu b'mitzvo-sechö,
v'kayrav-tönu malkaynu
la-avodö-sechö, v'shim'chö
ha-gödol v'haködosh ölaynu körösö.

15. אַתָּה בְחַרְתָּנוּ מִכָּל הָעַמִּים,
אָהַבְתָּ אוֹתָנוּ וְרָצִיתָ בָּנוּ,
וְרוֹמַמְתָּנוּ מִכָּל הַלְּשׁוֹנוֹת,
וְקִדַּשְׁתָּנוּ בְּמִצְוֹתֶיךָ,
וְקֵרַבְתָּנוּ מַלְכֵּנוּ
לַעֲבֹדָתֶךָ, וְשִׁמְךָ
הַגָּדוֹל וְהַקָּדוֹשׁ עָלֵינוּ קָרָאתָ.

You have chosen us from among all the nations; You have loved us and found favor with us. You have raised us above all tongues and made us holy through Your commandments. You, our King, have drawn us near to Your service and proclaimed Your great and holy Name upon us.

16. Ayleh chö-m'döh libi,   **16.** אֵלֶה חָמְדָה לִבִּי,
v'chusöh nö v'al tis-alaym.   וְחוּסָה נָא וְאַל תִּתְעַלֵּם.

These are the desires of my heart. Have mercy and turn not away from us.

17. Aylechö hashem ekrö, v'el   **17.** אֵלֶיךָ ה׳ אֶקְרָא, וְאֶל
hashem es-chanön. Sh'ma hashem   ה׳ אֶתְחַנָּן. שְׁמַע ה׳
v'chönayni, hashem he-yay ozayr li.   וְחָנֵּנִי, ה׳ הֱיֵה עֹזֵר לִי.

It is to You, Lord, that I call; it is the Lord to whom I appeal. Listen, O Lord, and be gracious to me; Lord, be my helper.

18. Ayleh vörechev v'ayleh va-susim,   **18.** אֵלֶה בָרֶכֶב וְאֵלֶה בַסּוּסִים,
va-anachnu b'shaym hashem nazkir.   וַאֲנַחְנוּ בְּשֵׁם ה׳ נַזְכִּיר.

Some rely on chariots, others on cavalry, but we invoke the name of the Lord.

19. Ayli-yöhu ha-növi, ayli-yöhu   **19.** אֵלִיָּהוּ הַנָּבִיא, אֵלִיָּהוּ
ha-tishbi, ayli-yöhu hagil-ödi,   הַתִּשְׁבִּי, אֵלִיָּהוּ הַגִּלְעָדִי,
bim'hayröh yövo aylaynu im   בִּמְהֵרָה יָבֹא אֵלֵינוּ עִם
möshi-ach ben dövid.   מָשִׁיחַ בֶּן דָּוִד.

Elijah the prophet, Elijah the Tishbi, Elijah the Gilodi, will swiftly come to us with Moshiach the son of David.

20. Aytz cha-yim hi lama-chazikim
böh, v'som'chehö m'ushör.
D'röchehö dar'chay no-am,
v'chöl n'sivosehö shölom.

20. עֵץ חַיִּים הִיא לַמַּחֲזִיקִים
בָּהּ, וְתֹמְכֶיהָ מְאֻשָּׁר.
דְּרָכֶיהָ דַרְכֵי נֹעַם,
וְכָל נְתִיבוֹתֶיהָ שָׁלוֹם.

It is a tree of life for those who hold fast to it, and those who support it are fortunate. Its ways are pleasant ways, and all its paths are peace.

21. Azamayr bish'vöchin, l'may-al
go pis-chin, d'vachakal ta-puchin,
d'inun ka-dishin.

21. אֲזַמֵּר בִּשְׁבָחִין, לְמֵיעַל
גּוֹ פִּתְחִין, דְּבַחֲקַל תַּפּוּחִין,
דְּאִנּוּן קַדִּישִׁין:

N'zamin löh hashtö, bif'sorö
chadatö, uvim'nartö tavtö,
d'nöhörö al rayshin.

נְזַמִּין לָהּ הַשְׁתָּא, בִּפְתוֹרָא
חַדָתָּא, וּבִמְנַרְתָּא טַבְתָּא,
דְּנָהֲרָא עַל רֵישִׁין:

Y'minö us'mölö, uvay-nai-hu chalöh,
b'kishutin öz'lö, umönin ul'vushin.

יְמִינָא וּשְׂמָאלָא, וּבֵינַיְהוּ כַלָּה,
בְּקִשּׁוּטִין אָזְלָא, וּמָאנִין וּלְבוּשִׁין:

Y'chabek löh ba-löh, uvi-sodö dilöh,
d'övayd nai-chö löh, y'hay
katish katishin.

יְחַבֵּק לָהּ בַּעְלָהּ, וּבִיסוֹדָא דִילָהּ,
דְּעָבֵד נַיְחָא לָהּ, יְהֵא
כָּתִישׁ כַּתִּישִׁין:

Tz'vöchin af aksin, b'taylin ush'visin,
b'ram anpin chadatin,

צְוָחִין אַף עַקְתִּין, בְּטֵלִין וּשְׁבִיתִין,
בְּרַם אַנְפִּין חֲדַתִּין,

99

v'ruchin im nafshin. :וְרוּחִין עִם נַפְשִׁין

Chadu sagay yaysay, v'al chadö
tartay, n'horö löh yimtay,
uvir'chö-ön din'fishin. חֲדוּ סַגִּי יֵיתֵי, וְעַל חֲדָא
תַּרְתֵּי, נְהוֹרָא לָהּ יִמְטֵי,
:וּבִרְכָאָן דִּנְפִישִׁין

K'rivu shush'vinin, avidu sikunin,
l'apöshö zinin, v'nunin im rachashin. קְרִיבוּ שׁוּשְׁבִינִין, עֲבִידוּ תִקּוּנִין,
:לְאַפָּשָׁא זִינִין, וְנוּנִין עִם רַחֲשִׁין

L'me-evad nish'mösin, v'ruchin
chadatin, b'sartayn uvis'lösin,
uvis'lösö shivshin. לְמֶעֱבַד נִשְׁמָתִין, וְרוּחִין
חֲדַתִּין, בְּתַרְתֵּין וּבִתְלָתִין,
:וּבִתְלָתָא שְׁבְשִׁין

V'iturin shav-in löh, umalkö
dil'aylö, d'yis-atar kolö,
b'kadish kadishin. וְעִטּוּרִין שַׁבְעִין לָהּ, וּמַלְכָּא
דִּלְעֵלָּא, דְּיִתְעַטַּר כֹּלָּא,
:בְּקַדִּישׁ קַדִּישִׁין

R'shimin us'simin, b'go köl ölmin,
b'ram atik yomin, halö
batish batishin. רְשִׁימִין וּסְתִימִין, בְּגוֹ כָּל עָלְמִין,
בְּרַם עַתִּיק יוֹמִין, הֲלָא
:בַּטִישׁ בַּטִישִׁין

Y'hay ra-avö kamayh, d'sishrayh al
amayh, d'yis-anag lish'mayh,
bim'sikin v'duvshin. יְהֵא רַעֲוָא קַמֵּהּ, דְּתִשְׁרֵיהּ עַל
עַמֵּהּ, דְּיִתְעַנַּג לִשְׁמֵהּ,
:בִּמְתִיקִין וְדוּבְשִׁין

100

Asadayr lid'romö, m'nartö dis'simö,   אֲסַדֵּר לִדְרוֹמָא, מְנַרְתָּא דִּסְתִימָא,

v'shulchön im na-hamö,   וְשֻׁלְחָן עִם נַהֲמָא,

bitz'fonö örshin.   בִּצְפוֹנָא אָרְשִׁין:

B'chamrö go chasö, um'dönay ösö,   בְּחַמְרָא גוֹ כַסָּא, וּמְדָּאנֵי אַסָּא,

l'örus va-arusöh, l'hasköföh chalöshin.   לְאָרוֹס וַאֲרוּסָה, לְהַתְקָפָה חַלָּשִׁין:

Na-avayd l'hon kisrin, b'milin ya-kirin,   נַעֲבֵיד לְהוֹן כִּתְרִין, בְּמִלִּין יַקִּירִין,

b'shav-in iturin, d'al gabay cham-shin.   בְּשַׁבְעִין עִטּוּרִין, דְּעַל גַּבֵּי חַמְשִׁין:

Sh'chintö tis-atör, b'shis na-hamay   שְׁכִינְתָּא תִּתְעַטָּר, בְּשִׁית נַהֲמֵי

lis'tör, b'vövin tiskatör,   לִסְטָר, בְּוָוִין תִּתְקַטָּר,

v'zinin dich'nishin.   וְזִינִין דִּכְנִישִׁין:

Sh'visin ush'vikin, m'sö-övin   שְׁבִיתִין וּשְׁבִיקִין, מְסָאֲבִין

dir'chikin, chavilin dim'ikin, v'chöl   דִּרְחִיקִין, חֲבִילִין דִּמְעִיקִין, וְכָל

zinay chavushin.   זִינֵי חֲבוּשִׁין:

L'miv-tza al riftö, k'zaysö   לְמִבְצַע עַל רִפְתָּא, כְּזֵיתָא

uch'vay-ösö, t'rayn yudin naktö,   וּכְבֵיעֲתָא, תְּרֵין יוּדִין נַקְטָא,

s'simin uf'rishin.   סְתִימִין וּפְרִישִׁין:

M'shach zaysö dach-yö, d'töchanin   מְשַׁח זֵיתָא דַכְיָא, דְּטָחֲנִין

raycha-yö, v'nagdin nachala-yö,   רֵיחַיָּא, וְנַגְדִּין נַחֲלַיָּא,

b'gavöh bil'chishin. : בְּגַוֵּהּ בִּלְחִישִׁין

Halö naymö rözin, umilin dig'nizin, הֲלָא נֵימָא רָזִין, וּמִלִּין דִּגְנִיזִין,
d'laysay-hon mis-chazin, דְּלֵיתֵיהוֹן מִתְחַזִּין,
t'mirin uch'vishin. : טְמִירִין וּכְבִישִׁין

Is-atöras kalöh, b'rözin dil'aylö, b'go אִתְעַטְּרַת כַּלָּה, בְּרָזִין דִּלְעֵלָּא, בְּגוֹ
hai hilulö, d'irin ka-dishin. : הַאי הִלּוּלָא, דְּעִירִין קַדִּישִׁין

Vi-hay ra-avö min ködöm a-tikö וִיהֵא רַעֲוָא מִן קֳדָם עַתִּיקָא
ka-dishö d'chöl ka-dishin, ut'mirö קַדִּישָׁא דְּכָל קַדִּישִׁין, וּטְמִירָא
d'chöl t'mirin s'simö d'cholö, דְּכָל טְמִירִין סְתִימָא דְּכֹלָּא,
d'yis-mashaych talö ilö-öh mi-nayh דְּיִתְמְשֵׁךְ טַלָּא עִלָּאָה מִנֵּיהּ
l'mal-yö rayshö diz'ayr anpin לְמַלְיָא רֵישָׁא דִּזְעֵיר אַנְפִּין
ul'hatil lachakal tapuchin וּלְהַטִּיל לַחֲקַל תַּפּוּחִין
kadishin bin'hiru d'anpin קַדִּישִׁין בִּנְהִירוּ דְּאַנְפִּין
b'ra-avö uv'chedvösö d'cholö. : בִּרְעֲוָא וּבְחֶדְוָתָא דְּכֹלָּא

I will cut away [the forces of evil] with songs of praise, in order to enter the holy gates of "Chakal Tapuchin." We herewith invite her [the Shechinah] to the festive table, with the beautiful candelabrum shining on our heads. Between right and left the Bride approaches, adorned in ornaments, jewels and robes.

22. B'chö böt'chu avosaynu, böt'chu va-t'fal'taymo. Aylechö zö-aku v'nimlötu, b'chö vöt'chu vlo voshu.

22. בְּךָ בָּטְחוּ אֲבֹתֵינוּ בָּטְחוּ וַתְּפַלְּטֵמוֹ: אֵלֶיךָ זָעֲקוּ וְנִמְלָטוּ, בְּךָ בָטְחוּ וְלֹא בוֹשׁוּ:

In You did our fathers trust, they trusted and You delivered them. To You did they cry, and they were removed from danger, they trusted in You and were not ashamed.

23. B'chö hashem chösisi al ay-voshöh l'olöm.

23. בְּךָ ה' חָסִיתִי אַל אֵבוֹשָׁה לְעוֹלָם.

In thee, O Lord, have I taken my refuge, that I shall not be ashamed forever.

24. Böruch hagever asher yivtach ba-shem, v'hö-yöh hashem mivtacho.

24. בָּרוּךְ הַגֶּבֶר אֲשֶׁר יִבְטַח בַּה', וְהָיָה ה' מִבְטַחוֹ.

Blessed is the man who trusts in the Lord, and the Lord will be his security.

25. Böruch hu elokaynu sheb'rö-önu lich'vodo, v'hivdilönu min ha-to-im, v'nösan lönu toras emes, v'cha-yay olöm nöta b'sochaynu.

25. בָּרוּךְ הוּא אֱלֹקֵינוּ שֶׁבְּרָאָנוּ לִכְבוֹדוֹ, וְהִבְדִּילָנוּ מִן הַתּוֹעִים, וְנָתַן לָנוּ תּוֹרַת אֱמֶת, וְחַיֵּי עוֹלָם נָטַע בְּתוֹכֵנוּ.

Blessed is our God Who created us for His glory, and has set us apart from those who go astray, and has given us the Torah of truth, and implanted within us eternal life.

26. Böruch kayl el-yon asher nösan
m'nuchö, l'naf-shaynu fid-yon mishays
va-anöchö, v'hu yidrosh l'tziyon ir
ha-nidöchö, ad önöh tug'yon
nefesh ne-enöchö.

בָּרוּךְ קֵל עֶלְיוֹן אֲשֶׁר נָתַן .26
מְנוּחָה, לְנַפְשֵׁנוּ פִּדְיוֹן מִשֵּׁאת
וַאֲנָחָה, וְהוּא יִדְרוֹשׁ לְצִיּוֹן עִיר
הַנִּדָּחָה, עַד אָנָה תּוּגְיוֹן
נֶפֶשׁ נֶאֱנָחָה :

Ha-shomayr shabös, ha-bayn im
ha-bas, lökayl yay-rö-tzu, k'min-chöh
al machavas.

הַשּׁוֹמֵר שַׁבָּת, הַבֵּן עִם
הַבַּת, לָקֵל יֵרָצוּ, כְּמִנְחָה
עַל מַחֲבַת :

Rochayv bö-arövos melech olömim,
es amo lishbos izayn ba-n'imim,
b'ma-achölay aray-vos b'minay
mat-amim, b'malbushay chövod
zevach mish-pöchöh. **Ha-shomayr**

רוֹכֵב בָּעֲרָבוֹת מֶלֶךְ עוֹלָמִים,
אֶת עַמּוֹ לִשְׁבּוֹת אִזֵּן בַּנְּעִימִים,
בְּמַאֲכָלֵי עֲרֵבוֹת בְּמִינֵי
מַטְעַמִּים, בְּמַלְבּוּשֵׁי כָבוֹד
זֶבַח מִשְׁפָּחָה : השומר

V'ashray köl cho-cheh l'sashlumay
chayfel, may-ays köl socheh sho-chayn
bö-aröfel, na-chalöh lo yizkeh böhör
uvashöfel, na-chalöh um'nuchöh
ka-shemesh lo zö-r'chöh. **Ha-shomayr**

וְאַשְׁרֵי כָּל חוֹכֶה לְתַשְׁלוּמֵי
כֵפֶל, מֵאֵת כָּל סוֹכֶה שׁוֹכֵן
בָּעֲרָפֶל, נַחֲלָה לוֹ יִזְכֶּה בָּהָר
וּבַשָּׁפֶל, נַחֲלָה וּמְנוּחָה
כַּשֶּׁמֶשׁ לוֹ זָרְחָה : השומר

Köl sho-mayr shabös kadös
may-cha-l'lo, hayn hech-shayr chibas

כָּל שׁוֹמֵר שַׁבָּת כַּדָּת
מֵחַלְּלוֹ, הֵן הֻכְשַׁר חִבַּת

kodesh go-rölo, v'im yö-tzö chovas
ha-yom ashray lo, el kayl ödon
m'cho-l'lo, min-chöh hi sh'luchöh.
Ha-shomayr

קֹדֶשׁ גּוֹרָלוֹ, וְאִם יָצָא חוֹבַת
הַיּוֹם אַשְׁרֵי לוֹ, אֵל קֵל אָדוֹן
מְחוֹלְלוֹ מִנְחָה הִיא שְׁלוּחָה: הַשּׁוֹמֵר

Chemdas ha-yömim k'rö-o kayli tzur,
v'ashray lis'mimim im yih-yeh nötzur,
keser hi-lumim al ro-shöm yötzur,
tzur hö-olömim rucho vöm nöchö.
Ha-shomayr

חֶמְדַּת הַיָּמִים קְרָאוֹ קֵלִי צוּר,
וְאַשְׁרֵי לִתְמִימִים אִם יִהְיֶה נָצוּר,
כֶּתֶר הִלּוּמִים עַל רֹאשָׁם יָצוּר,
צוּר הָעוֹלָמִים רוּחוֹ בָם נָחָה: הַשּׁוֹמֵר

Zöchor es yom ha-shabös l'kad'sho,
karno ki göv'höh nayzer al rosho, al
kayn yitayn hö-ödöm l'nafsho, oneg
v'gam simchöh böhem l'mösh-chöh.
Ha-shomayr

זָכוֹר אֶת יוֹם הַשַּׁבָּת לְקַדְּשׁוֹ,
קַרְנוֹ כִּי גָבְהָה נֵזֶר עַל רֹאשׁוֹ, עַל
כֵּן יִתֵּן הָאָדָם לְנַפְשׁוֹ, עוֹנֶג
וְגַם שִׂמְחָה בָּהֶם לְמָשְׁחָה: הַשּׁוֹמֵר

Kodesh hi löchem shabös ha-malköh,
el toch bötaychem l'höni-ach
b'röchöh, b'chöl mo-sh'vo-saychem
lo sa-asu m'lö-chöh, b'naychem
uv'nosay-chem, eved v'gam shifchöh.
Ha-shomayr

קֹדֶשׁ הִיא לָכֶם שַׁבָּת הַמַּלְכָּה,
אֶל תּוֹךְ בָּתֵּיכֶם לְהָנִיחַ
בְּרָכָה, בְּכָל מוֹשְׁבוֹתֵיכֶם
לֹא תַעֲשׂוּ מְלָאכָה, בְּנֵיכֶם
וּבְנוֹתֵיכֶם עֶבֶד וְגַם שִׁפְחָה: הַשּׁוֹמֵר:

Blessed is God Who gives our weary souls rest. God commanded us to make the Shabbat a a special day and we will be amply rewarded for it. Remember to keep the Shabbat holy; revel in its royal splendor. Let the Shabbat Queen bring blessing into your home.

27. D'ror yikrö l'vayn im bas,
v'yin-tzör'chem k'mo vövas, n'im
shim'chem v'lo yush-bas, sh'vu
v'nuchu b'yom shabös.

27. דְּרוֹר יִקְרָא לְבֵן עִם בַּת,
וְיִנְצָרְכֶם כְּמוֹ בָבַת, נְעִים
שִׁמְכֶם וְלֹא יֻשְׁבַּת, שְׁבוּ
וְנוּחוּ בְּיוֹם שַׁבָּת.

D'rosh növi v'ulömi, v'os yesha a-say
imi, n'ta sorayk b'soch karmi,
sh'ay shav-as b'nay ami.

דְּרוֹשׁ נָוִי וְאוּלָמִי, וְאוֹת יֶשַׁע עֲשֵׂה
עִמִּי, נְטַע שׂוֹרֵק בְּתוֹךְ כַּרְמִי,
שְׁעֵה שַׁוְעַת בְּנֵי עַמִּי.

D'roch puröh b'soch bötz-röh, v'gam
bövel asher gö-v'röh, n'sotz tzörai b'af
v'evröh, sh'ma koli b'yom ekrö.

דְּרוֹךְ פּוּרָה בְּתוֹךְ בָּצְרָה, וְגַם
בָּבֶל אֲשֶׁר גָּבְרָה, נְתוֹץ צָרַי בְּאַף
וְעֶבְרָה, שְׁמַע קוֹלִי בְּיוֹם אֶקְרָא.

Elokim tayn ba-midbör har, hadas
shitöh b'rosh tid-hör, v'lamaz-hir
v'laniz-hör, sh'lomim tayn
k'may nöhör.

אֱלֹקִים תֵּן בַּמִּדְבָּר הַר, הֲדַס
שִׁטָּה בְּרוֹשׁ תִּדְהָר, וְלַמַּזְהִיר
וְלַנִּזְהָר, שְׁלוֹמִים תֵּן
כְּמֵי נָהָר.

Hadoch kömay kayl kanö, b'mog
layvöv uvam'ginöh, v'nar-chiv peh
un'mal'enöh, l'shonaynu l'chö rinöh.

הֲדוֹךְ קָמַי קֵל קַנָּא, בְּמוֹג
לֵבָב וּבַמְּגִנָּה, וְנַרְחִיב פֶּה
וּנְמַלְאֶנָּה, לְשׁוֹנֵנוּ לְךָ רִנָּה.

106

D'ay chöchmöh l'nafshe-chö, v'hi   דְּעֵה חָכְמָה לְנַפְשֶׁךָ, וְהִיא

cheser l'ro-shechö, n'tzor   כֶתֶר לְרֹאשֶׁךָ, נְצוֹר

mitzvas k'doshechö, sh'mor   מִצְוַת קְדוֹשֶׁךָ, שְׁמוֹר

shabas köd-shechö.   שַׁבַּת קָדְשֶׁךָ.

God provides protection for us; praise Him unceasingly and keep the Shabbat. May God restore the Holy Temple and answer the prayer of His people. May He crush our enemies and send the redeemer. May He grant peace to those who keep the Shabbat.

28. Ilu ho-tzi-önu   אִלוּ הוֹצִיאָנוּ .28

mimitzra-yim da-yaynu.   מִמִּצְרַיִם דַּיֵּנוּ.

Had He [only] brought us out of Egypt, it would have sufficed us.

29. Dövid melech yisrö-ayl   דָּוִד מֶלֶךְ יִשְׂרָאֵל .29

chai v'ka-yöm.   חַי וְקַיָּם.

David, King of Israel, is living and enduring.

30. Esö aynai el hehörim. may-ayin   אֶשָּׂא עֵינַי אֶל הֶהָרִים, מֵאַיִן .30

yövo ezri. Ezri may-im hashem,   יָבוֹא עֶזְרִי. עֶזְרִי מֵעִם ה',

osay shöma-yim vö-öretz.   עֹשֵׂה שָׁמַיִם וָאָרֶץ.

I lift my eyes to the mountains — from where will my help come? My help will come from the Lord, Maker of heaven and earth.

31. Ha-vayn yakir li efra-yim, im   הֲבֵן יַקִּיר לִי אֶפְרַיִם, אִם .31

yeled sha-ashu-im, ki miday dab'ri   יֶלֶד שַׁעֲשׁוּעִים, כִּי מִדֵּי דַבְּרִי

bo, zöchor ez-k'renu od.   בּוֹ זָכֹר אֶזְכְּרֶנּוּ עוֹד.

[Is] Ephraim [not] My beloved son, is he not a precious child that whenever I speak of him I recall him even more?

32. Ha-l'lu es hashem köl go-yim, shab'chuhu köl hö-umim. Ki gövar ölaynu chasdo, ve-emes hashem l'olöm, ha-l'luköh.

32. הַלְלוּ אֶת ה׳ כָּל גּוֹיִם, שַׁבְּחוּהוּ כָּל הָאֻמִּים. כִּי גָבַר עָלֵינוּ חַסְדּוֹ, וֶאֱמֶת ה׳ לְעוֹלָם, הַלְלוּיָהּ.

Praise the Lord, all you nations; extol Him, all you peoples. For His kindness was mighty over us, and the truth of the Lord is everlasting. Praise the Lord.

33. Harninu laylokim uzaynu, hö-ri-u laylokay ya-akov. S'u zimröh us'nu sof, kinor nö-im im növel.

33. הַרְנִינוּ לֵאלֹקִים עוּזֵּנוּ, הָרִיעוּ לֵאלֹקֵי יַעֲקֹב. שְׂאוּ זִמְרָה וּתְנוּ תֹף, כִּנּוֹר נָעִים עִם נָבֶל.

Sing joyously to God, our strength, shout for joy to the God of Jacob. Take up the hymn; sound the drum, the pleasant harp and the lute.

34. Hashem z'chörönu y'vöraych, y'vöraych es bays yisrö-ayl, y'vöraych es bays aharon. Y'voraych yir'ay hashem, ha-k'tanim im hag'dolim. Yosayf hashem alaychem, alaychem v'al b'naychem. B'ruchim atem la-shem, osay shöma-yim vö-öretz. Ha-shöma-yim shö-ma-yim la-shem, v'hö-öretz nösan liv'nay ödöm. Lo ha-maysim y'ha-l'lu köh, v'lo köl yor'day dumöh. Va-anachnu

34. ה׳ זְכָרָנוּ יְבָרֵךְ, יְבָרֵךְ אֶת בֵּית יִשְׂרָאֵל, יְבָרֵךְ אֶת בֵּית אַהֲרֹן. יְבָרֵךְ יִרְאֵי ה׳, הַקְּטַנִּים עִם הַגְּדֹלִים. יֹסֵף ה׳ עֲלֵיכֶם, עֲלֵיכֶם וְעַל בְּנֵיכֶם. בְּרוּכִים אַתֶּם לַה׳, עֹשֵׂה שָׁמַיִם וָאָרֶץ. הַשָּׁמַיִם שָׁמַיִם לַה׳, וְהָאָרֶץ נָתַן לִבְנֵי אָדָם. לֹא הַמֵּתִים יְהַלְלוּ קָהּ, וְלֹא כָּל יוֹרְדֵי דוּמָה. וַאֲנַחְנוּ

108

n'vöraych köh, may-atöh v'ad נְבָרֵךְ קָהּ, מֵעַתָּה וְעַד
olöm, ha-l'luköh. עוֹלָם, הַלְלוּקָהּ.

The Lord Who is ever mindful of us, may He bless: May He bless the House of Israel; may He bless the House of Aaron; may He bless those who fear the Lord, the small with the great. May the Lord increase [blessing] upon you, upon you and upon your children. You are blessed by the Lord, the Maker of heaven and earth. The heavens are the Lord's heavens, but the earth He gave to the children of man. The dead cannot praise the Lord, nor any who descend into the silence [of the grave]. But we will bless the Lord from now to eternity. Praise the Lord.

35. Ha-tov ki lo chölu ra-chamechö, 35. הַטּוֹב כִּי לֹא כָלוּ רַחֲמֶיךָ,
v'ham'rachaym ki lo samu וְהַמְרַחֵם כִּי לֹא תַמּוּ
chasödechö, ki may-olöm חֲסָדֶיךָ, כִּי מֵעוֹלָם
kivinu löch. קִוִּינוּ לָךְ:

You are the Beneficent One, for Your mercies never cease; the Merciful One, for Your kindnesses never end; for we always place our hope in You.

36. Hinay mah tov umah nö-im 36. הִנֵּה מַה טּוֹב וּמַה נָּעִים
sheves achim gam yöchad. שֶׁבֶת אַחִים גַּם יָחַד.

How good and pleasant it is when brothers live together in harmony.

37. Hörachamön hu yan-chilaynu 37. הָרַחֲמָן הוּא יַנְחִילֵנוּ
l'yom shekulo shabös um'nuchöh לְיוֹם שֶׁכֻּלּוֹ שַׁבָּת וּמְנוּחָה
l'cha-yay hö-olömim. לְחַיֵּי הָעוֹלָמִים.

May the Merciful One let us inherit that day which will be all Shabbat and rest for life everlasting.

38. Hörachamön hu yishlach lönu
es ayli-yöhu hanövi zöchur latov,
vi-vaser lönu b'soros tovos
y'shu-os v'nechömos.

38. הָרַחֲמָן הוּא יִשְׁלַח לָנוּ
אֶת אֵלִיָּהוּ הַנָּבִיא זָכוּר לַטּוֹב,
וִיבַשֶּׂר לָנוּ בְּשׂוֹרוֹת טוֹבוֹת
יְשׁוּעוֹת וְנֶחָמוֹת.

May the Merciful One send us Elijah the prophet — may he be remembered for good — and let him bring us good tidings, deliverance and consolation.

39. Hoshi-öh es amechö, uvöraych
es nachalösechö, ur'aym
v'nas'aym ad hö-olöm.

39. הוֹשִׁיעָה אֶת עַמֶּךָ, וּבָרֵךְ
אֶת נַחֲלָתֶךָ, וּרְעֵם
וְנַשְּׂאֵם עַד הָעוֹלָם.

Save Your people and bless Your possession; tend them and sustain them forever.

40. Hu elokaynu hu övinu, hu
malkaynu, hu moshi-aynu, hu
yoshi-aynu v'yig-ölaynu shaynis
b'körov, v'yashmi-aynu b'rachamöv
l'aynay köl chai laymor: Hayn gö-alti
es'chem acharis kiv'rayshis lih-yos
löchem laylokim.

40. הוּא אֱלֹקֵינוּ הוּא אָבִינוּ, הוּא
מַלְכֵּנוּ, הוּא מוֹשִׁיעֵנוּ, הוּא
יוֹשִׁיעֵנוּ וְיִגְאָלֵנוּ שֵׁנִית
בְּקָרוֹב, וְיַשְׁמִיעֵנוּ בְּרַחֲמָיו
לְעֵינֵי כָּל חַי לֵאמֹר: הֵן גָּאַלְתִּי
אֶתְכֶם אַחֲרִית כְּבְרֵאשִׁית לִהְיוֹת
לָכֶם לֵאלֹקִים.

He is our God; He is our Father; He is our King; He is our Deliverer. He will soon again save and redeem us, and in His mercy will let us hear, in the sight of every living thing, as follows: Behold, I have redeemed you from this final [exile] as from the first, to be your God.

41. Im atem m'sham'rim nayros
shel shabös, ani mar-eh löchem
nayros shel tziyon.

‏41. אִם אַתֶּם מְשַׁמְּרִים נֵרוֹת
שֶׁל שַׁבָּת, אֲנִי מַרְאֶה לָכֶם
נֵרוֹת שֶׁל צִיּוֹן.‏

If you uphold the Lights of Shabbat, then I will show you the Lights of Zion.

42. Im ömarti mötöh ragli,
chasd-chö hashem yis-ödayni. B'rov
sar-apai b kirbi, tanchumechö
y'sha-ash'u nafshi.

‏42. אִם אָמַרְתִּי מָטָה רַגְלִי,
חַסְדְּךָ ה' יִסְעָדֵנִי. בְּרֹב
שַׂרְעַפַּי בְּקִרְבִּי, תַּנְחוּמֶיךָ
יְשַׁעַשְׁעוּ נַפְשִׁי.‏

When I thought that my foot was slipping, Your kindness, O Lord, supported me. When my [worrisome] thoughts multiply within me, Your consolation delights my soul.

43. Ivdu es hashem b'simchöh, bo-u
l'fönöv bir'nönöh. Ki tov hashem
l'olöm chasdo, v'ad dor
vödor emunöso.

‏43. עִבְדוּ אֶת ה' בְּשִׂמְחָה, בֹּאוּ
לְפָנָיו בִּרְנָנָה. כִּי טוֹב ה'
לְעוֹלָם חַסְדּוֹ, וְעַד דֹּר
וָדֹר אֱמוּנָתוֹ.‏

Serve the Lord with joy; come before Him with exultation. For the Lord is good; His kindness is everlasting, and His faithfulness is for all generations.

44. K'a-yöl ta-arog al afikay mö-yim,
kayn nafshi sa-arog ay-lechö elokim.
Tzö-m'oh nafshi lay-lokim l'kayl chöy,
mösai övo v'ayrö-eh p'nay elokim.

‏44. כְּאַיָּל תַּעֲרֹג עַל אֲפִיקֵי מָיִם,
כֵּן נַפְשִׁי תַעֲרֹג אֵלֶיךָ אֱלֹקִים.
צָמְאָה נַפְשִׁי לֵאלֹקִים לְקֵל חָי,
מָתַי אָבוֹא וְאֵרָאֶה פְּנֵי אֱלֹקִים.‏

As the hart pants for the water brooks so my soul longs for You, Oh Lord. My soul thirsts for the living God; when will I come and appear before God?

45. Kayl hahodö-os adon hashölom,   ‎45. קֵל הַהוֹדָאוֹת אֲדוֹן הַשָּׁלוֹם,
m'kadaysh ha-shabös um'öraych   ‎מְקַדֵּשׁ הַשַּׁבָּת וּמְבָרֵךְ
sh'vi-i, umayni-ach bik'dushöh l'am   ‎שְׁבִיעִי, וּמֵנִיחַ בִּקְדֻשָּׁה לְעַם
m'dush'nay oneg, zaycher   ‎מְדֻשְּׁנֵי עֹנֶג, זֵכֶר
l'ma-asay v'rayshis.   ‎לְמַעֲשֵׂה בְרֵאשִׁית.

He is the God worthy of thanks, the Master of peace, Who sanctifies the Shabbat and blesses the Seventh Day and brings rest with holiness to a people satiated with delight – in remembrance of the work of Creation.

46. Kayl n'kömos hashem, kayl   ‎46. קֵל נְקָמוֹת ה', קֵל
n'kömos hofi-a. Hinösay shofayt   ‎נְקָמוֹת הוֹפִיעַ. הִנָּשֵׂא שֹׁפֵט
hö-öretz, höshayv g'mul al gay-im.   ‎הָאָרֶץ, הָשֵׁב גְּמוּל עַל גֵּאִים.
La-shem ha-y'shu-öh, al am'chö   ‎לַה' הַיְשׁוּעָה, עַל עַמְּךָ
vir'chösechö selöh.   ‎בִרְכָתֶךָ סֶּלָה.

The Lord is a God of retribution; O God of retribution, reveal Yourself! Judge of the earth, arise; render to the arrogant their recompense. Deliverance is the Lord's; may Your blessing be upon Your people forever.

47. Kayli atöh v'odekö,   ‎47. קֵלִי אַתָּה וְאוֹדֶךָּ,
elokai aro-m'mekö.   ‎אֱלֹקַי אֲרוֹמְמֶךָּ.

You are my God and I will praise You, my God – and I will exalt You.

48. Kay-tzad m'rak'dim lif'nay   ‎48. כֵּיצַד מְרַקְּדִים לִפְנֵי
ha-kalöh, kalöh nö-öh vachasudöh.   ‎הַכַּלָּה, כַּלָּה נָאָה וַחֲסוּדָה.

What does one say when dancing before a bride? "The bride is beautiful and virtuous."

49. Ki elokim yoshi-a tziyon
v'yivneh öray y'hudöh v'yösh'vu
shöm viray-shuhö. V'zera avödöv
yin-chöluhö v'ohavay sh'mo
yish-k'nu vöh.

49. כִּי אֱלֹקִים יוֹשִׁיעַ צִיּוֹן
וְיִבְנֶה עָרֵי יְהוּדָה וְיָשְׁבוּ
שָׁם וִירֵשׁוּהָ. וְזֶרַע עֲבָדָיו
יִנְחָלוּהָ וְאֹהֲבֵי שְׁמוֹ
יִשְׁכְּנוּ בָהּ.

For God will give salvation to Zion and build the cities of Judah; they shall abide there and shall take possession of it once more. The seed of His servants shall inherit it, and those that love His Name shall find their dwelling place therein.

50. Ki haym cha-yaynu v'orech
yömaynu, uvöhem neh-geh yomöm
völöy-löh, v'ahavös'chö lo sösur
mimenu l'olömim.

50. כִּי הֵם חַיֵּינוּ וְאֹרֶךְ
יָמֵינוּ, וּבָהֶם נֶהְגֶּה יוֹמָם
וָלָיְלָה, וְאַהֲבָתְךָ לֹא תָסוּר
מִמֶּנּוּ לְעוֹלָמִים.

For they are our life and the length of our days, and we will meditate on them day and night. May Your love never depart from us.

51. Ki l'chö tov l'hodos, ul'shim'chö
nö-eh l'zamayr. Ki may-olöm v'ad
olöm atöh kayl.

51. כִּי לְךָ טוֹב לְהוֹדוֹת, וּלְשִׁמְךָ
נָאֶה לְזַמֵּר. כִּי מֵעוֹלָם וְעַד
עוֹלָם אַתָּה קֵל.

It is good to give thanks to You and pleasant to sing praises to Your Name, for You are God forever.

52. Ki lo yitosh hashem amo,
v'nachalöso lo ya-azov. Hashem
hoshi-öh, hamelech ya-anaynu
v'yom kör'aynu.

52. כִּי לֹא יִטֹּשׁ ה' עַמּוֹ,
וְנַחֲלָתוֹ לֹא יַעֲזֹב. ה'
הוֹשִׁיעָה, הַמֶּלֶךְ יַעֲנֵנוּ
בְיוֹם קָרְאֵנוּ.

Indeed, the Lord will not abandon His people, nor will He forsake His heritage. Deliver us, O Lord; may the King answer us on the day we call.

53. Ki mitziyon tay-tzay soröh, ud'var hashem mi-rushölö-yim.

‫53. כִּי מִצִּיּוֹן תֵּצֵא תוֹרָה,‬
‫וּדְבַר ה' מִירוּשָׁלָיִם.‬

For from Zion shall go forth the Torah, and the word of the Lord from Jerusalem.

54. Ki v'simchöh say-tzay-u uv'shölom tuvölun, he-hörim v'hag'vö-os yif-tz'chu lif-naychem ri-nöh v'chöl atzay ha-södeh yim-cha-u chöf.

‫54. כִּי בְשִׂמְחָה תֵצֵאוּ‬
‫וּבְשָׁלוֹם תּוּבָלוּן, הֶהָרִים‬
‫וְהַגְּבָעוֹת יִפְצְחוּ לִפְנֵיכֶם‬
‫רִנָּה וְכָל עֲצֵי הַשָּׂדֶה‬
‫יִמְחֲאוּ כָף.‬

For you will go out joyfully and be led forth peacefully. Mountains and hills will burst into song before you, and all the trees will clap hands.

55. Ko ömar hashem, zöcharti löch chesed n'ura-yich, ahavas k'lulo-sö-yich, lech-taych acha-rai ba-midbör b'eretz lo z'ruöh.

‫55. כֹּה אָמַר ה', זָכַרְתִּי לָךְ‬
‫חֶסֶד נְעוּרַיִךְ, אַהֲבַת‬
‫כְּלוּלֹתָיִךְ, לֶכְתֵּךְ אַחֲרַי‬
‫בַּמִּדְבָּר בְּאֶרֶץ לֹא זְרוּעָה:‬

Thus said the Lord, I remember for you the devotion of your youth, the love of your bridal days, as you went after Me in the wilderness, in an uncultivated land.

56. Köh ribon ölam v'öl'ma-yö, ant hu malkö melech mal-cha-yö, ovad g'vur-taych v'sim-hayö, sh'far

‫56. קָה רִבּוֹן עָלַם וְעָלְמַיָּא, אַנְתְּ‬
‫הוּא מַלְכָּא מֶלֶךְ מַלְכַיָּא, עוֹבַד‬
‫גְּבוּרְתֵּךְ וְתִמְהַיָּא, שְׁפַר‬

ködömöch l'hachavö-yö.	קְדָמָךְ לְהַחֲוָיָא.

Sh'vochin asadayr tzafrö v'ramshö, löch elökö ka-dishö di v'rö köl naf-shö, irin kadishin uv'nay enöshö, chayvas börö v'ofay sh'ma-yö. **Köh ribon ölam**	שְׁבָחִין אֲסַדֵּר צַפְרָא וְרַמְשָׁא, לָךְ אֱלָקָא קַדִּישָׁא דִּי בְרָא כָל נַפְשָׁא, עִירִין קַדִּישִׁין וּבְנֵי אֱנָשָׁא, חֵיוַת בָּרָא וְעוֹפֵי שְׁמַיָּא. קָה רִבּוֹן עָלַם...

Rav-r'vin ov'daych v'sakifin, möchich r'ma-yö v'zakif k'fifin, lu yich-yeh g'var sh'nin al'fin, lö yay-ol g'vurtaych b'chush-b'na-yö. **Köh ribon ölam**	רַבְרְבִין עוֹבְדֵיךְ וְתַקִּיפִין, מָכִיךְ רְמַיָּא וְזַקִּיף כְּפִיפִין, לוּ יִחְיֶה גְּבַר שְׁנִין אַלְפִין, לָא יֵעוֹל גְּבוּרְתֵּךְ בְּחֻשְׁבְּנַיָּא. קָה רִבּוֹן עָלַם...

Elökö di layh y'kar ur'vusö, p'rok yas önöch mipum ar-y'vösö, v'apayk yas amaych migo gölusö, amaych di v'chart miköl uma-yö. **Köh ribon ölam**	אֱלָקָא דִּי לֵהּ יְקַר וּרְבוּתָא, פְּרוֹק יַת עָנָךְ מִפּוּם אַרְיְוָתָא, וְאַפֵּיק יַת עַמֵּךְ מִגּוֹ גָלוּתָא, עַמֵּךְ דִּי בְחַרְתְּ מִכָּל אֻמַּיָּא. קָה רִבּוֹן עָלַם...

L'mikdöshaych tuv ul'kodesh kud-shin, asar di vayh yechedun ruchin v'nafshin, vizam'run löch shirin v'rachashin, bi-rush'laym kartö d'shuf-ra-yö. **Köh ribon ölam**	לְמִקְדָּשֵׁךְ תּוּב וּלְקֹדֶשׁ קֻדְשִׁין, אֲתַר דִּי בֵהּ יֶחֱדוּן רוּחִין וְנַפְשִׁין, וִיזַמְּרוּן לָךְ שִׁירִין וְרַחֲשִׁין, בִּירוּשְׁלֵם קַרְתָּא דְשׁוּפְרַיָּא. קָה רִבּוֹן עָלַם...

Lord of all worlds! All Your creatures praise You. Even if we lived a thousand years, we could not recount the extent of Your greatness. God, save Your people from their exile and rebuild the Temple, and there, in Jerusalem, we will really be able to sing to You!

57. Köl hö-olöm kulo gesher tzar m'od. V'hö-ikör lo l'fachayd k'löl.

‏57. כָּל הָעוֹלָם כֻּלּוֹ גֶּשֶׁר צַר מְאֹד. וְהָעִקָּר לֹא לְפַחֵד כְּלָל.

The whole world is a very narrow bridge, but the main thing is not to fear at all.

58. Layv töhor b'rö li elokim, v'ru-ach nöchon cha-daysh b'kirbi. Al tashli-chayni mil'fönechö, v'ru-ach köd-sh'chö al tikach mi-meni.

‏58. לֵב טָהוֹר בְּרָא לִי אֱלֹקִים, וְרוּחַ נָכוֹן חַדֵּשׁ בְּקִרְבִּי. אַל תַּשְׁלִיכֵנִי מִלְּפָנֶיךָ, וְרוּחַ קָדְשְׁךָ אַל תִּקַּח מִמֶּנִּי:

Create in me a pure heart, O God, and renew within me an upright spirit. Do not cast me out of Your presence, and do not take Your Spirit of Holiness away from me.

59. L'ma-an achai v'ray-öy, adab'röh nö sholom böch. L'ma-an bays hashem elokaynu, avak'shöh tov löch.

‏59. לְמַעַן אַחַי וְרֵעָי, אֲדַבְּרָה נָּא שָׁלוֹם בָּךְ. לְמַעַן בֵּית ה׳ אֱלֹקֵינוּ, אֲבַקְשָׁה טוֹב לָךְ.

For the sake of my brethren and friends, I ask that there be peace within you. For the sake of the House of the Lord our God, I seek your well-being.

60. Lo yisö goy el goy cherev v'lo yil-m'du od milchömöh.

‏60. לֹא יִשָּׂא גוֹי אֶל גּוֹי חֶרֶב וְלֹא יִלְמְדוּ עוֹד מִלְחָמָה.

Nation will not lift sword against nation, and they will no longer learn of war.

61. L'shönöh habö-öh **61. לְשָׁנָה הַבָּאָה**
bi-rushöla-yim ha-b'nuyöh. **בִּירוּשָׁלַיִם הַבְּנוּיָה.**

Next year in the rebuilt Jerusalem.

62. Lulay he-emanti lir-os **62. לוּלֵא הֶאֱמַנְתִּי לִרְאוֹת**
b'tuv hashem b'eretz cha-yim. **בְּטוּב ה' בְּאֶרֶץ חַיִּים.**

If I had not believed that I would see the goodness of the Lord in the land of the living [they would have crushed me]!

63. La-y'hudim hö-y'söh o-röh **63. לַיְּהוּדִים הָיְתָה אוֹרָה**
v'simchöh, v'söson vikör. **וְשִׂמְחָה, וְשָׂשׂוֹן וִיקָר.**
Kayn tih'yeh lönu. **כֵּן תִּהְיֶה לָּנוּ.**

For the Jews there was light and joy, gladness and honor—so let it be with us.

64. Mipi kayl, mipi kayl, **64. מִפִּי קֵל, מִפִּי קֵל,**
y'vöraych es yisrö-ayl. **יְבָרֵךְ אֶת יִשְׂרָאֵל.**

Ayn adir ka-shem, v'ayn böruch **אֵין אַדִּיר כַּה', וְאֵין בָּרוּךְ**
k'ven amröm, v'ayn g'dulöh **כְּבֶן עַמְרָם, וְאֵין גְּדֻלָה**
ka-toröh, v'ayn dor'shöh **כַּתּוֹרָה, וְאֵן דּוֹרְשָׁה**
k'yisrö-ayl. **Mipi kayl** **כְּיִשְׂרָאֵל. מִפִּי קֵל.**

Ayn hödur ka-shem, v'ayn **אֵין הָדוּר כַּה', וְאֵין**
vösik k'ven amröm, **וָתִיק כְּבֶן עַמְרָם,**

v'ayn zakö-öh ka-toröh,	וְאֵין זַכָּאָה כַּתּוֹרָה,
v'ayn chom'döh k'yisrö-ayl.	וְאֵין חוֹמְדָּה כְּיִשְׂרָאֵל.
Mipi kayl	מִפִּי קֵל

Ayn töhor ka-shem, v'ayn yöshör	אֵין טָהוֹר כַּה', וְאֵין יָשָׁר
k'ven amröm, v'ayn k'vudöh	כְּבֶן עַמְרָם, וְאֵין כְּבוּדָּה
ka-toröh, v'ayn lom'döh	כַּתּוֹרָה, וְאֵן לוֹמְדָה
k'yisrö-ayl. Mipi kayl	כְּיִשְׂרָאֵל. מִפִּי קֵל

Ayn melech ka-shem, v'ayn növi	אֵין מֶלֶךְ כַּה', וְאֵין נָבִיא
k'ven amröm, v'ayn som'chöh	כְּבֶן עַמְרָם, וְאֵין סוֹמְכָה
ka-toröh, v'ayn oz'röh	כַּתּוֹרָה, וְאֵין עוֹזְרָה
k'yisrö-ayl. Mipi kayl	כְּיִשְׂרָאֵל. מִפִּי קֵל

Ayn po-deh ka-shem, v'ayn tzadik	אֵין פּוֹדֶה כַּה', וְאֵין צַדִּיק
k'ven amröm, v'ayn k'doshöh	כְּבֶן עַמְרָם, וְאֵין קְדוֹשָׁה
ka-toröh, v'ayn rocha-shö	כַּתּוֹרָה, וְאֵין רוֹחֲשָׁה
k'yisrö-ayl. Mipi kayl	כְּיִשְׂרָאֵל. מִפִּי קֵל

Ayn sho-mayr ka-shem,	אֵין שׁוֹמֵר כַּה',
v'ayn tömim k'ven amröm,	וְאֵין תָּמִים כְּבֶן עַמְרָם,
v'ayn t'mimöh ka-toröh, v'ayn	וְאֵין תְּמִימָה כַּתּוֹרָה, וְאֵין
tom'chöh k'yisrö-ayl. Mipi kayl	תוֹמְכָה כְּיִשְׂרָאֵל. מִפִּי קֵל

From the mouth of God, Israel is blessed. There is no splendor like that of

God, and no one is blessed like Moses; [there is] no greatness greater than the Torah; and no learners [of the Torah] like Israel.

65. Mal'chus'chö mal'chus köl
olömim, umem-shal-t'chö
b'chöl dor vödor.

65. מַלְכוּתְךָ מַלְכוּת כָּל
עוֹלָמִים, וּמֶמְשַׁלְתְּךָ
בְּכָל דּוֹר וָדֹר.

Your kingship is a kingship over all worlds, and Your dominion is throughout all generations.

66. Mi hu zeh, v'ay zeh hu,
zeh kayli v'an-vayhu.

66. מִי הוּא זֶה וְאֵי זֶה הוּא,
זֶה קֵלִי וְאַנְוֵהוּ.

Who is He, and where is He? This is my God, and I will glorify Him.

67. Mikolos ma-yim rabim
adirim mish-b'ray yöm
adir bamörom hashem.

67. מִקֹּלוֹת מַיִם רַבִּים
אַדִּירִים מִשְׁבְּרֵי יָם
אַדִּיר בַּמָּרוֹם ה'.

More than the sound of mighty waters, than the mighty breakers of the sea, is the Lord mighty on high.

68. Mimitzra-yim g'altönu,
mibays avödim p'disönu.

68. מִמִּצְרַיִם גְּאַלְתָּנוּ,
מִבֵּית עֲבָדִים פְּדִיתָנוּ.

You have delivered us from Egypt, redeemed us from the house of bondage.

69. Min ha-maytzar körösi köh,
önöni vamerchöv köh.

69. מִן הַמֵּצַר קָרָאתִי קָּה,
עָנָנִי בַמֶּרְחָב קָּה.

From out of distress I called to God; with abounding relief, God answered me.

70. M'kimi may-öför döl.

70. מְקִימִי מֵעָפָר דָּל.

He raises the poor from the dust.

71. M'nuchöh v'simchöh or la-y'hudim, yom shaböson yom machama-dim, shom'röv v'zoch'röv hay-möh m'idim, ki l'shishöh kol b'ru-im v'om'dim.

71. מְנוּחָה וְשִׂמְחָה אוֹר לַיְּהוּדִים, יוֹם שַׁבָּתוֹן יוֹם מַחֲמַדִּים, שׁוֹמְרָיו וְזוֹכְרָיו הֵמָּה מְעִידִים, כִּי לְשִׁשָּׁה כֹּל בְּרוּאִים וְעוֹמְדִים.

Sh'may shöma-yim eretz v'yamim, köl tz'vö mörom g'vohim v'römim, tanin v'ödöm v'cha-yas r'aymim, ki b'köh Hashem tzur olömim.

שְׁמֵי שָׁמַיִם אֶרֶץ וְיַמִּים, כָּל צְבָא מָרוֹם גְּבוֹהִים וְרָמִים, תַּנִּין וְאָדָם וְחַיַּת רְאֵמִים, כִּי בְּקָהּ ה' צוּר עוֹלָמִים.

Hu asher diber l'am s'gulöso, shömor l'kad'sho mibo-o v'ad tzayso, shabas kodesh yom chemdöso, ki vo shövas kayl miköl m'lachto.

הוּא אֲשֶׁר דִּבֶּר לְעַם סְגֻלָּתוֹ, שָׁמוֹר לְקַדְּשׁוֹ מִבּוֹאוֹ וְעַד צֵאתוֹ, שַׁבַּת קֹדֶשׁ יוֹם חֶמְדָּתוֹ, כִּי בוֹ שָׁבַת קֵל מִכָּל מְלַאכְתּוֹ.

B'mitzvas shabös kayl yachali-tzöch, kum k'rö aylöv yöchish l'am'tzöch, nish'mas köl chai v'gam na-ari-tzöch, echol b'simchöh ki ch'vör rö-tzöch.

בְּמִצְוֹת שַׁבָּת קֵל יַחֲלִיצָךְ, קוּם קְרָא אֵלָיו יָחִישׁ לְאַמְּצָךְ, נִשְׁמַת כָּל חַי וְגַם נַעֲרִיצָךְ, אֱכוֹל בְּשִׂמְחָה כִּי כְבָר רָצָךְ.

B'mishneh lechem v'kidush raböh,

בְּמִשְׁנֶה לֶחֶם וְקִדּוּשׁ רַבָּה,

b'rov mat-amim v'ru-ach n'divöh, בְּרֹב מַטְעַמִּים וְרוּחַ נְדִיבָה,

yizku l'rav tuv hamis-an'gim böh, יִזְכּוּ לָרַב טוּב הַמִּתְעַנְּגִים בָּהּ,

b'vi-as go-ayl l'cha-yay hö-olöm habö. בְּבִיאַת גּוֹאֵל לְחַיֵּי הָעוֹלָם הַבָּא.

By observing Shabbat, we acknowledge that the world and all that it contains were created by God in six days. Everything is special on Shabbat, from the prayers we recite to the food we eat, two loaves of bread and the Kiddush wine. Those who enjoy it will be richly rewarded with the coming of the Moshiach.

72. Mo-deh ani l'fönechö, melech chai v'ka-yöm, she-hechezartö bi nish'mösi b'chemlöh. Raböh emunö-sechö.

72. מוֹדֶה אֲנִי לְפָנֶיךָ, מֶלֶךְ חַי וְקַיָּם, שֶׁהֶחֱזַרְתָּ בִּי נִשְׁמָתִי בְּחֶמְלָה. רַבָּה אֱמוּנָתֶךָ.

I offer thanks to You, living and eternal King, for You have mercifully restored my soul within me; Your faithfulness is great.

73. Nöchon libi, elokim, nöchon libi, öshirö va-azamay-röh. Uröh ch'vodi, uröh ha-nayvel v'chinor, ö-iröh shöchar.

73. נָכוֹן לִבִּי אֱלֹקִים נָכוֹן לִבִּי, אָשִׁירָה וַאֲזַמֵּרָה. עוּרָה כְבוֹדִי, עוּרָה הַנֵּבֶל וְכִנּוֹר, אָעִירָה שָּׁחַר.

My heart is resolute, God, my heart is resolute. I will sing and chant praises. Awake, O my honor; awake, O psalter and harp; I shall awake the dawn.

74. Nodöh bihudöh elokim
b'yisrö-ayl gödol sh'mo.
Va-y'hi v'shölaym suko
um'onöso v'tziyon.

74. נוֹדָע בִּיהוּדָה אֱלֹקִים
בְּיִשְׂרָאֵל גָּדוֹל שְׁמוֹ.
וַיְהִי בְשָׁלֵם סֻכּוֹ
וּמְעוֹנָתוֹ בְצִיּוֹן.

In Judah God is recognized; His name has become great throughout Israel.
When His tabernacle was in Shalem and His dwelling place in Zion.

75. N'ye zhuritzi chlöptzi, tshtö
s'nami bu-dyet, mi pö-yedem
na kar-tsh-yönki tam ee
vödka bu-dyet.

75. נְיֶע זשׁוּרִיטצִי כְלָאפְצִי טשׁטָא
סְנַאמִי בּוּדְיֶעט, מִי פָּאיֶעדֶעם
נָא קַארְטשׁיָאנְקִי טַאם אִי
וָאדְקָא בּוּדְיֶעט.

Don't worry fellows of what will become of us. We will travel to an inn
(place of learning); there will surely be what to drink there (Torah).

76. Od yishöma b'öray y'hudöh
uv'chutzos y'rushölö-yim, kol söson
v'kol simchöh, kol chösön
v'kol kalöh.

76. עוֹד יִשָּׁמַע בְּעָרֵי יְהוּדָה
וּבְחוּצוֹת יְרוּשָׁלָיִם, קוֹל שָׂשׂוֹן
וְקוֹל שִׂמְחָה, קוֹל חָתָן
וְקוֹל כַּלָּה.

May there still be heard in the cities of Judah and in the streets of Jerusalem
the sound of joy and the sound of happiness, the sound of a groom and the
sound of a bride.

77. Or zöru-a la-tzadik,
ul'yish'ray layv simchöh.

77. אוֹר זָרֻעַ לַצַּדִּיק,
וּלְיִשְׁרֵי לֵב שִׂמְחָה.

Light is sown for the righteous, and joy for the upright in heart.

78. O-seh shölom bim'romöv,
hu ya-aseh shölom ölaynu,
v'al köl yisrö-ayl v'im'ru ömayn.

‏78. עֹשֶׂה שָׁלוֹם בִּמְרוֹמָיו,‏
‏הוּא יַעֲשֶׂה שָׁלוֹם עָלֵינוּ,‏
‏וְעַל כָּל יִשְׂרָאֵל וְאִמְרוּ אָמֵן.‏

He Who makes peace in His heavens, may He make peace for us and for all Israel; and say, Amen.

79. Öshiröh la-shem b'cha-yöy
azam'röh laylokai b'odi. Ye-erav ölöv
sichi önochi es-mach ba-shem.
Yitamu chatö-im min hö-öretz
ur'shö-im od aynöm, bö-r'chi nafshi
es hashem, ha-l'luköh.

‏79. אָשִׁירָה לַה׳ בְּחַיָּי‏
‏אֲזַמְּרָה לֵאלֹקַי בְּעוֹדִי. יֶעֱרַב עָלָיו‏
‏שִׂיחִי אָנֹכִי אֶשְׂמַח בַּה׳.‏
‏יִתַּמּוּ חַטָּאִים מִן הָאָרֶץ‏
‏וּרְשָׁעִים עוֹד אֵינָם, בָּרְכִי נַפְשִׁי‏
‏אֶת ה׳, הַלְלוּקָהּ.‏

I will sing to the Lord with my soul; I will chant praise to my God with my [entire] being. May my prayer be pleasant to Him; I will rejoice in the Lord. May sinners cease from the earth, and the wicked be no more. Bless the Lord, O my soul! Praise the Lord.

80. Övinu malkaynu ayn lönu
melech elö ötöh.

‏80. אָבִינוּ מַלְכֵּנוּ אֵין לָנוּ‏
‏מֶלֶךְ אֶלָּא אָתָּה.‏

Our Father, our King, we have no King but You.

81. Övinu malkaynu chönaynu
va-anaynu ki ayn bönu ma-asim,
asay imönu tz'dököh vöchesed
v'hoshi-aynu.

‏81. אָבִינוּ מַלְכֵּנוּ חָנֵּנוּ‏
‏וַעֲנֵנוּ כִּי אֵין בָּנוּ מַעֲשִׂים,‏
‏עֲשֵׂה עִמָּנוּ צְדָקָה וָחֶסֶד‏
‏וְהוֹשִׁיעֵנוּ.‏

Our Father, our King, be gracious to us and answer us, for we have no meritorious deeds; for the sake of Your great Name, deal charitably and kindly with us and deliver us.

82. Övinu öv hörachamön,
ha-m'rachaym, rachem nö ölaynu,
v'sayn b'libaynu binöh l'hövin
ul'haskil, lishmo-a lilmod
ul'lamayd, lishmor v'la-asos,
ul'ka-yaym es köl div'ray salmud
torösechö b'ahavöh. V'hö-ayr
aynaynu b'sorösechö, v'dabayk
libaynu b'mitzvosechö, v'yachayd
l'vövaynu l'ahavöh ul'yir-öh
es sh'mechö.

‏82. אָבִינוּ אָב הָרַחֲמָן,‏
‏הַמְרַחֵם, רַחֵם נָא עָלֵינוּ,‏
‏וְתֵן בְּלִבֵּנוּ בִּינָה לְהָבִין‏
‏וּלְהַשְׂכִּיל, לִשְׁמֹעַ לִלְמֹד‏
‏וּלְלַמֵּד, לִשְׁמֹר וְלַעֲשׂוֹת,‏
‏וּלְקַיֵּם אֶת כָּל דִּבְרֵי תַלְמוּד‏
‏תּוֹרָתֶךָ בְּאַהֲבָה. וְהָאֵר‏
‏עֵינֵינוּ בְּתוֹרָתֶךָ, וְדַבֵּק‏
‏לִבֵּנוּ בְּמִצְוֹתֶיךָ, וְיַחֵד‏
‏לְבָבֵנוּ לְאַהֲבָה וּלְיִרְאָה‏
‏אֶת שְׁמֶךָ.‏

Our Father, merciful Father Who is compassionate, have mercy on us, and grant our heart understanding to comprehend and to discern, to perceive, to learn and to teach, to observe, to practice and to fulfill all the teachings of Your Torah with love. Enlighten our eyes in Your Torah, cause our hearts to cleave to Your commandments, and unite our hearts to love and fear your Name.

83. Övo big'vuros hashem elokim
azkir tzid'kös'chö l'vadechö.

‏83. אָבוֹא בִּגְבֻרוֹת ה' אֱלֹקִים‏
‏אַזְכִּיר צִדְקָתְךָ לְבַדֶּךָ.‏

I will come with strength O God, I will mention Your righteousness, Yours alone.

84. Pis'chu li sha-aray tzedek, ‏84. פִּתְחוּ לִי שַׁעֲרֵי צֶדֶק,‏
övo vöm o-deh köh. ‏אָבֹא בָם אוֹדֶה קָהּ.‏

Open for me the gates of righteousness; I will enter them and praise God.

85. Rachamönö d'önay la-ani-yay ‏85. רַחֲמָנָא דְעָנֵי לַעֲנִיֵּי‏
anaynö. Rachamönö d'önay ‏עֲנֵינָא. רַחֲמָנָא דְעָנֵי‏
lis'viray libö anaynö. ‏לִתְבִירֵי לִבָּא עֲנֵינָא.‏

May the Merciful One, Who answers the poor, answer us. May the Merciful One, Who answers the broken-hearted, answer us.

86. Rachaym b'chasdechö, al amchö ‏86. רַחֵם בְּחַסְדְּךָ, עַל עַמְּךָ‏
tzuraynu, al tziyon mishkan ‏צוּרֵנוּ, עַל צִיּוֹן מִשְׁכַּן‏
k'vodechö, z'vul bays tif-artaynu. ‏כְּבוֹדֶךָ, זְבוּל בֵּית תִּפְאַרְתֵּנוּ,‏
Ben dövid avdechö, yövo ‏בֶּן דָּוִד עַבְדְּךָ, יָבֹא‏
v'yig-ölaynu, ru-ach apaynu, ‏וְיִגְאָלֵנוּ, רוּחַ אַפֵּינוּ,‏
m'shi-ach hashem. ‏מְשִׁיחַ ה׳.‏

With Your kindness, have mercy, upon Israel Your people, upon Zion the abode of Your glory, the abode of the House of our glory. The son of David, Your servant, will come and redeem us, the spirit of our mouths, the anointed one of God.

87. Ro-m'mu hashem elokaynu ‏87. רוֹמְמוּ ה׳ אֱלֹקֵינוּ‏
v'hish-tachavu l'har köd-sho, ‏וְהִשְׁתַּחֲווּ לְהַר קָדְשׁוֹ,‏
ki ködosh hashem elokaynu. ‏כִּי קָדוֹשׁ ה׳ אֱלֹקֵינוּ:‏

Exalt the Lord our God, and bow down at His holy mountain, for the Lord our God is holy.

88. Samach t'samach ray-im
hö-ahuvim k'samay-chachö y'tzir'chö
b'gan ayden mikedem.

88. שַׂמֵּחַ תְּשַׂמַּח רֵעִים
הָאֲהוּבִים כְּשַׂמֵּחֲךָ יְצִירְךָ
בְּגַן עֵדֶן מִקֶּדֶם.

Grant abundant joy to these loving friends, as You bestowed gladness upon Your created being in the Garden of Eden of old.

89. She-yibö-neh bays hamikdösh
bim'hayröh v'yömaynu, v'sayn
chelkaynu b'sorösechö.

89. שֶׁיִּבָּנֶה בֵּית הַמִּקְדָּשׁ
בִּמְהֵרָה בְיָמֵינוּ, וְתֵן
חֶלְקֵנוּ בְּתוֹרָתֶךָ.

[May it be your will] that the Beis Hamikdosh be speedily rebuilt in our days, and grant us our portion in Your Torah.

90. Sh'ma yisrö-ayl, hashem
elokaynu, hashem echöd.

90. שְׁמַע יִשְׂרָאֵל, ה׳
אֱלֹקֵינוּ, ה׳ אֶחָד.

Hear, O Israel, the Lord is our God, the Lord is One.

91. Sh'sulim b'vays hashem
b'chatz'ros elokaynu yaf-richu.
Od y'nuvun b'sayvöh d'shaynim
v'ra-ananim yih-yu. L'hagid ki
yöshör hashem tzuri v'lo avlösö bo.

91. שְׁתוּלִים בְּבֵית ה׳
בְּחַצְרוֹת אֱלֹקֵינוּ יַפְרִיחוּ.
עוֹד יְנוּבוּן בְּשֵׂיבָה דְּשֵׁנִים
וְרַעֲנַנִּים יִהְיוּ. לְהַגִּיד כִּי
יָשָׁר ה׳ צוּרִי וְלֹא עַוְלָתָה בּוֹ.

Planted in the House of the Lord, they shall blossom in the courtyards of our God. They shall be fruitful even in old age; they shall be full of sap and freshness. That is to say that the Lord is just; He is my strength, and there is no injustice in Him.

92. Sim shölom tovöh uv'röchöh,
cha-yim chayn vöchesed v'rachamim,
ölaynu v'al köl yisrö-ayl amechö.
Bö-r'chaynu övinu kulönu k'echöd
b'or pönechö, ki v'or pönechö nösató
lönu, hashem elokaynu, toras
cha-yim v'ahav chesed utz'dököh
uv'röchöh v'rachamim
v'cha-yim v'shölom.

‎92. שִׂים שָׁלוֹם טוֹבָה וּבְרָכָה,
חַיִּים חֵן וָחֶסֶד וְרַחֲמִים,
עָלֵינוּ וְעַל כָּל יִשְׂרָאֵל עַמֶּךָ.
בָּרְכֵנוּ אָבִינוּ כֻּלָּנוּ כְּאֶחָד
בְּאוֹר פָּנֶיךָ, כִּי בְאוֹר פָּנֶיךָ נָתַתָּ
לָנוּ, ה' אֱלֹקֵינוּ, תּוֹרַת
חַיִּים וְאַהֲבַת חֶסֶד וּצְדָקָה
וּבְרָכָה וְרַחֲמִים
וְחַיִּים וְשָׁלוֹם.

Bestow peace, goodness and blessing, life, graciousness, kindness and mercy, upon us and upon all Your people Israel. Bless us, our Father, all of us as one, with the light of Your countenance. For by the light of Your countenance You gave us, Lord our God, the Torah of life and loving-kindness, righteousness, blessing, mercy, life and peace.

93. Simön tov umazöl tov y'hay
lönu ul'chöl yisrö-ayl ömayn.

‎93. סִמָּן טוֹב וּמַזָּל טוֹב יְהֵא
לָנוּ וּלְכָל יִשְׂרָאֵל אָמֵן.

May there be a good omen and good mazal for us and for all Israel. Amen.

94. S'u sh'örim röshaychem, us'u
pis'chay olöm, v'yövo melech
ha-kövod. Mi hu zeh melech
ha-kövod, hashem tz'vö-kos, hu
melech ha-kövod selöh.

‎94. שְׂאוּ שְׁעָרִים רָאשֵׁיכֶם, וּשְׂאוּ
פִּתְחֵי עוֹלָם, וְיָבֹא מֶלֶךְ
הַכָּבוֹד. מִי הוּא זֶה מֶלֶךְ
הַכָּבוֹד, ה' צְבָקוֹת, הוּא
מֶלֶךְ הַכָּבוֹד סֶלָה.

Lift up your heads, O gates; lift them up, eternal doors, so the glorious King may enter. Who is the glorious King? The Lord of hosts, He is the glorious King for all eternity.

95. T'ra-naynöh s'fösai ki azam'röh löch v'nafshi asher pödisö.   95. תְּרַנֵּנָּה שְׂפָתַי כִּי אֲזַמְּרָה לָךְ וְנַפְשִׁי אֲשֶׁר פָּדִיתָ.

My lips shall rejoice when I sing unto You, and my soul which You have redeemed.

96. Toröh tzivöh lönu moshe, moröshöh k'hilas ya-akov.   96. תּוֹרָה צִוָּה לָנוּ מֹשֶׁה, מוֹרָשָׁה קְהִלַּת יַעֲקֹב.

The Torah which Moses commanded us is the heritage of the Congregation of Jacob.

97. Tzavay y'shu-os ya-akov.   97. צַוֵּה יְשׁוּעוֹת יַעֲקֹב.

Give the command for the salvation of Jacob.

98. Tziyon halo sish-ali lish'lom asira-yich.   98. צִיּוֹן הֲלֹא תִשְׁאֲלִי לִשְׁלוֹם אֲסִירָיִךְ.

O Zion, why are you not concerned with the welfare of your prisoners?

99. Tzö-m'öh l'chö nafshi kömah l'chö v'söri b'eretz tziyöh v'ö-yayf b'li mö-yim. Kayn ba-kodesh chazi-sichö lir-os uz'chö uch'vodechö.   99. צָמְאָה לְךָ נַפְשִׁי כָּמַהּ לְךָ בְשָׂרִי בְּאֶרֶץ צִיָּה וְעָיֵף בְּלִי מָיִם. כֵּן בַּקֹּדֶשׁ חֲזִיתִךְ לִרְאוֹת עֻזְּךָ וּכְבוֹדֶךָ.

My soul thirsts for You; my flesh longs for You, in a dry and weary land where no water is; so I look for You in the sanctuary, to see Your power and Your glory.

100. Tzur mishelo öchalnu bö-r'chu
emunai, söva-nu v'hosarnu
kid'var hashem.

צוּר מִשֶּׁלּוֹ אָכַלְנוּ בָּרְכוּ .100
אֱמוּנַי, שָׂבַעְנוּ וְהוֹתַרְנוּ
כִּדְבַר ה'.

Hazön es olömo ro-aynu övinu,
öchalnu es lachmo v'yayno shösinu,
al kayn no-deh lish'mo un'ha-l'lo
b'finu, ömarnu v'öninu ayn
ködosh ka-shem. **Tzur mishelo**

הַזָּן אֶת עוֹלָמוֹ רוֹעֵנוּ אָבִינוּ,
אָכַלְנוּ אֶת לַחְמוֹ וְיֵינוֹ שָׁתִינוּ,
עַל כֵּן נוֹדֶה לִשְׁמוֹ וּנְהַלְלוֹ
בְּפִינוּ, אָמַרְנוּ וְעָנִינוּ אֵין
קָדוֹשׁ כַּה'. צוּר מִשֶּׁלּוֹ

B'shir v'kol todöh n'vöraych
laylo-kaynu, al eretz chemdöh tovöh
shehin-chil la-avosaynu, mözon
v'tzaydöh hisbi-a l'nafshaynu, chasdo
govar ölaynu ve-emes hashem.
Tzur mishelo

בְּשִׁיר וְקוֹל תּוֹדָה נְבָרֵךְ
לֵאלֹקֵינוּ, עַל אֶרֶץ חֶמְדָּה טוֹבָה
שֶׁהִנְחִיל לַאֲבוֹתֵינוּ, מָזוֹן
וְצֵדָה הִשְׂבִּיעַ לְנַפְשֵׁנוּ, חַסְדוֹ
גָּבַר עָלֵינוּ וֶאֱמֶת ה'.
צוּר מִשֶּׁלּוֹ

Rachaym b'chasdechö al am'chö
tzuraynu, al tziyon mishkan
k'vodechö z'vul bays tif-artaynu, ben
dövid avdechö yövo v'yig-ölaynu,
ru-ach apaynu m'shi-ach hashem.
Tzur mishelo

רַחֵם בְּחַסְדֶּךָ עַל עַמְּךָ
צוּרֵנוּ, עַל צִיּוֹן מִשְׁכַּן
כְּבוֹדֶךָ זְבוּל בֵּית תִּפְאַרְתֵּנוּ, בֶּן
דָּוִד עַבְדֶּךָ יָבוֹא וְיִגְאָלֵנוּ,
רוּחַ אַפֵּינוּ מְשִׁיחַ ה'.
צוּר מִשֶּׁלּוֹ

Yibö-neh hamikdösh, ir tziyon
t'malay, v'shöm nöshir shir chödösh
uvir'nönöh na-aleh, hörachamön
hanikdösh yisbörach v'yis-aleh, al kos
ya-yin mölay k'virkas hashem.

יִבָּנֶה הַמִּקְדָּשׁ, עִיר צִיּוֹן
תְּמַלֵּא, וְשָׁם נָשִׁיר שִׁיר חָדָשׁ
וּבִרְנָנָה נַעֲלֶה, הָרַחֲמָן
הַנִּקְדָּשׁ יִתְבָּרַךְ וְיִתְעַלֶּה, עַל כּוֹס
יַיִן מָלֵא כְּבִרְכַּת ה'.

Tzur mishelo   צוּר מִשֶּׁלּוֹ

My friends, let us bless God, whose food we have eaten. He feeds the world and deserves our praise. God, have mercy on us and send the Moshiach. Rebuild the Temple and we will sing a new song over a cup brimming with wine.

101. Uföratz-tö yömöh vökayd-möh
v'tzöfonöh vö-negböh.

101. וּפָרַצְתָּ יָמָּה וָקֵדְמָה
וְצָפֹנָה וָנֶגְבָּה.

And you shall spread forth to the west, and to the east, and to the north, and to the south.

102. Ush'avtem ma-yim b'söson
mima-a-y'nay ha-y'shu-öh.

102. וּשְׁאַבְתֶּם מַיִם בְּשָׂשׂוֹן
מִמַּעַיְנֵי הַיְשׁוּעָה.

You shall draw water with joy from the wellsprings of deliverance.

103. Uv'chayn tzadikim yir-u
v'yis-möchu, vishörim ya-alozu,
va-chasidim b'rinöh yögilu.

103. וּבְכֵן צַדִּיקִים יִרְאוּ
וְיִשְׂמָחוּ, וִישָׁרִים יַעֲלֹזוּ,
וַחֲסִידִים בְּרִנָּה יָגִילוּ.

And then the righteous will see and be glad, the upright will rejoice, and the pious will exult in song.

104. Uv'nay y'rushöla-yim ir 　　　　**104. וּבְנֵה יְרוּשָׁלַיִם עִיר**
ha-kodesh bim'hayröh v'yömaynu. 　　**הַקֹּדֶשׁ בִּמְהֵרָה בְיָמֵינוּ.**

And rebuild Jerusalem the holy city speedily in our days.

105. V'chol ma-aminim she-hu chai 　**105. וְכֹל מַאֲמִינִים שֶׁהוּא חַי**
v'ka-yöm, ha-tov umaytiv 　　　　　**וְקַיָּם, הַטּוֹב וּמֵטִיב**
lörö-im v'la-tovim. 　　　　　　　　**לָרָעִים וְלַטּוֹבִים.**

Everyone acknowledges that He lives and endures; He is good and benevolent to both the wicked and the good people.

106. Va-harikosi löchem b'röchö 　　**106. וַהֲרִיקֹתִי לָכֶם בְּרָכָה**
ad b'li döy, ad she-yivlu 　　　　　**עַד בְּלִי דָי, עַד שֶׁיִּבְלוּ**
sif'so-saychem mi-lomar dai. 　　　**שִׂפְתוֹתֵיכֶם מִלּוֹמַר דַּי.**

I will bestow upon you blessings, [in such abundance] until your lips will become sore from saying [we have] enough.

107. V'hö-ayr aynay-nu b'sorösechö 　**107. וְהָאֵר עֵינֵינוּ בְּתוֹרָתֶךָ**
v'dabayk li-baynu b'mitzvo-sechö, 　**וְדַבֵּק לִבֵּנוּ בְּמִצְוֹתֶיךָ,**
v'yachayd l'vövaynu l'ahavöh 　　　**וְיַחֵד לְבָבֵנוּ לְאַהֲבָה**
ul'yir-öh es sh'mechö. V'lo nayvosh, **וּלְיִרְאָה אֶת שְׁמֶךָ. וְלֹא נֵבוֹשׁ,**
v'lo nikölaym, v'lo niköshayl l'olöm **וְלֹא נִכָּלֵם, וְלֹא נִכָּשֵׁל, לְעוֹלָם**
vö-ed. Ki v'shaym köd-sh'chö 　　　**וָעֶד. כִּי בְשֵׁם קָדְשְׁךָ**
ha-gödol v'ha-norö bötöch-nu, 　　**הַגָּדוֹל וְהַנּוֹרָא בָטָחְנוּ,**
nögilö v'nis-m'chö bishu-ösechö. 　**נָגִילָה וְנִשְׂמְחָה בִּישׁוּעָתֶךָ.**

Enlighten our eyes in Your Torah, cause our hearts to cleave to Your commandments, and unite our hearts to love and fear Your Name, and may we never be put to shame, disgrace or stumbling. Because we trust in Your holy, great and awesome Name, may we rejoice and exult in Your salvation.

108. V'hö-yöh ba-yom hahu yitöka b'shoför gödol, uvö-u hö-ov'dim b'eretz ashur v'hanidöchim b'eretz mitzrö-yim. V'hish-tachavu la-shem b'har ha-kodesh bi-rushölö-yim.

108. וְהָיָה בַּיוֹם הַהוּא יִתָּקַע בְּשׁוֹפָר גָּדוֹל, וּבָאוּ הָאֹבְדִים בְּאֶרֶץ אַשּׁוּר וְהַנִּדָּחִים בְּאֶרֶץ מִצְרָיִם. וְהִשְׁתַּחֲווּ לַה' בְּהַר הַקֹּדֶשׁ בִּירוּשָׁלָיִם.

And it shall be on that day, that a great shofar shall be sounded, and those who were lost in the land of Ashur and those banished in the land of Mitzrayim shall come and bow to the Lord on the holy mountain in Jerusalem.

109. V'chöl kar'nay r'shö-im agaday-a t'romam-nöh kar'nos tzadik. O-y'vöv albish boshes v'ölöv yö-tzitz nizro.

109. וְכָל קַרְנֵי רְשָׁעִים אֲגַדֵּעַ תְּרוֹמַמְנָה קַרְנוֹת צַדִּיק. אוֹיְבָיו אַלְבִּישׁ בֹּשֶׁת וְעָלָיו יָצִיץ נִזְרוֹ.

I shall cut down all the horns of the lawless, so that the horn of the righteous may rise up. His enemies I will clothe with shame, but upon himself his crown will blossom.

110. Vaylokim malki mi-kedem po-ayl y'shu-os b'kerev hö-öretz.

110. וֵאלֹקִים מַלְכִּי מִקֶּדֶם פֹּעֵל יְשׁוּעוֹת בְּקֶרֶב הָאָרֶץ.

And yet God is my King from the days of old, the purposeful Creator of manifold works of the salvation in the midst of the earth.

111. V'hi she-öm'döh la-avosaynu
v'lönu, shelo echöd bil'vöd ömad
ölaynu l'chalo-saynu, elö sheb'chöl
dor vödor om'dim ölaynu
l'chalo-saynu, v'haködosh
böruch hu matzilaynu mi-yödöm.

111. וְהִיא שֶׁעָמְדָה לַאֲבוֹתֵינוּ
וְלָנוּ, שֶׁלֹּא אֶחָד בִּלְבָד עָמַד
עָלֵינוּ לְכַלּוֹתֵנוּ, אֶלָּא שֶׁבְּכָל
דּוֹר וָדוֹר עוֹמְדִים עָלֵינוּ
לְכַלּוֹתֵנוּ, וְהַקָּדוֹשׁ
בָּרוּךְ הוּא מַצִּילֵנוּ מִיָּדָם.

It is this that has stood by our fathers and us. For not only one has risen against us to annihilate us, but in every generation they rise against us to annihilate us. But the Holy One, Blessed be He, rescues us from their hand.

112. V'hö-yu lim'shisöh shosö-yich
v'röchaku köl m'val'öyich. Yösis
öla-yich elokö-yich kim'sos
chösön al kalöh.

112. וְהָיוּ לִמְשִׁסָּה שֹׁאסָיִךְ
וְרָחֲקוּ כָּל מְבַלְּעָיִךְ. יָשִׂישׂ
עָלַיִךְ אֱלֹקַיִךְ כִּמְשׂוֹשׂ
חָתָן עַל כַּלָּה.

Those who despoil you will be despoiled, and all who would destroy you will be far away. Your God will rejoice over you as a bridegroom rejoices over his bride.

113. V'körayv p'zuraynu mibayn
hago-yim, un'fu-tzosaynu
kanays miyar-k'say öretz.

113. וְקָרֵב פְּזוּרֵינוּ מִבֵּין
הַגּוֹיִם, וּנְפוּצוֹתֵינוּ
כַּנֵּס מִיַּרְכְּתֵי אָרֶץ.

Gather our dispersed from among the nations, and assemble our scattered from the ends of the earth.

114. V'li-rushöla-yim ir'chö
b'rachamim töshuv, v'sishkon
b'sochöh ka-asher dibartö, uv'nay
osöh b'körov b'yömaynu binyan
olöm, v'chisay dövid avd'chö
m'hayröh b'sochöh töchin.

114. וְלִירוּשָׁלַיִם עִירְךָ
בְּרַחֲמִים תָּשׁוּב, וְתִשְׁכּוֹן
בְּתוֹכָהּ כַּאֲשֶׁר דִּבַּרְתָּ, וּבְנֵה
אוֹתָהּ בְּקָרוֹב בְּיָמֵינוּ בִּנְיַן
עוֹלָם, וְכִסֵּא דָוִד עַבְדְּךָ
מְהֵרָה בְּתוֹכָהּ תָּכִין.

Return in mercy to Jerusalem Your city and dwell therein as You have promised; and rebuild it, soon in our days, as an everlasting edifice, and speedily establish therein the throne of David Your servant.

115. V'nikaysi dömöm lo nikaysi,
va-shem shochayn b'tziyon.

115. וְנִקֵּיתִי דָּמָם לֹא נִקֵּיתִי,
וַה׳ שֹׁכֵן בְּצִיּוֹן.

I will cleanse [the nations of their wrongdoings], but for the [shedding of Jewish] blood I will not cleanse them; the Lord dwells in Zion.

116. V'sömach-tö b'chagechö
v'hö-yisö ach sömay-ach.

116. וְשָׂמַחְתָּ בְּחַגֶּךָ
וְהָיִיתָ אַךְ שָׂמֵחַ.

Rejoice in your Festival, and you shall be altogether joyful.

117. V'ya-azor v'yögayn v'yoshi-a
l'chöl hachosim bo.

117. וְיַעֲזוֹר וְיָגֵן וְיוֹשִׁיעַ
לְכָל הַחוֹסִים בּוֹ.

May He help, shield and redeem all those who turn to Him for refuge.

118. Y'did nefesh öv höra-chamön,
m'shoch av-d'chö el r'tzonechö,

118. יְדִיד נֶפֶשׁ אָב הָרַחֲמָן,
מְשׁוֹךְ עַבְדְּךָ אֶל רְצוֹנֶךָ,

yörutz av-d'chö k'mo a-yöl,
yish-tachaveh el mul ha-dörechö,
ye-erav lo y'didosechö, minofes
tzuf v'chöl tö-am.

יָרוּץ עַבְדְּךָ כְּמוֹ אַיָּל,
יִשְׁתַּחֲוֶה אֶל מוּל הֲדָרֶךָ,
יֶעֱרַב לוֹ יְדִידוֹתֶיךָ, מִנּוֹפֶת
צוּף וְכָל טָעַם.

Hödur nö-eh ziv hö-olöm, nafshi
cholas ahavösechö, önö kayl nö r'fö
nö löh, b'har-os löh no-am zivechö,
öz tis-cha-zayk v'sis-rapay, v'hö-y'söh
löh simchas olöm.

הָדוּר נָאֶה זִיו הָעוֹלָם, נַפְשִׁי
חוֹלַת אַהֲבָתֶךָ, אָנָא קֵל נָא רְפָא
נָא לָה, בְּהַרְאוֹת לָה נוֹעַם זִיוֶךָ,
אָז תִּתְחַזֵּק וְתִתְרַפֵּא, וְהָיְתָה
לָה שִׂמְחַת עוֹלָם.

Vösik ye-hemu racha-mechö, v'chusö
nö al bayn ahuvechö, ki zeh kamöh
nich-sof nich-safti lir-os b'sif-eres
uzechö, ayleh chö-m'döh libi
v'chusöh nö v'al tis-alöm.

וָתִיק יֶהֱמוּ רַחֲמֶיךָ, וְחוּסָה
נָא עַל בֵּן אֲהוּבֶךָ, כִּי זֶה כַּמָּה
נִכְסוֹף נִכְסַפְתִּי לִרְאוֹת בְּתִפְאֶרֶת
עֻזֶּךָ, אֵלֶּה חָמְדָה לִבִּי
וְחוּסָה נָא וְאַל תִּתְעַלָּם.

Higö-leh nö uf'ros chavivi ölai es
sukas sh'lomechö, tö-ir eretz
mik'vodechö, nögilöh v'nis'm'chöh
böch, ma-hayr öhuv ki vö mo-ayd,
v'chönaynu kimay olöm.

הִגָּלֶה נָא וּפְרוֹס חֲבִיבִי עָלַי אֶת
סֻכַּת שְׁלוֹמֶךָ, תָּאִיר אֶרֶץ
מִכְּבוֹדֶךָ, נָגִילָה וְנִשְׂמְחָה
בָּךְ, מַהֵר אָהוּב כִּי בָא מוֹעֵד,
וְחָנֵּנוּ כִּימֵי עוֹלָם.

Beloved of [my] soul, merciful Father, draw Your servant to Your will. [Then]
Your servant will run as swiftly as a deer; he will bow before Your splendor;

*Your acts of affection will be sweeter than honeycomb and every pleasant
taste. Glorious, resplendent One, Light of the world, my soul is lovesick for
You; I beseech You, O God, pray heal it by showing it the sweetness of Your
splendor. Then it will be strengthened and healed and will experience
everlasting joy. O pious One, may Your mercy be aroused and have
compassion upon Your beloved child. For it is long that I have been
yearning to behold the glory of Your majesty. These my heart desires, so
have pity and do not conceal Yourself. Reveal Yourself, my Beloved, and
spread over me the shelter of Your peace. Let the earth be illuminated by
Your glory; we will rejoice and exult in You. Hasten, Beloved, for the time
has come; and be gracious unto us as in days of yore.*

119. Ya-aleh tachanu-naynu may-erev,   יַעֲלֶה תַּחֲנוּנֵנוּ מֵעֶרֶב,

v'yövo shav-ösaynu mi-boker,   וְיָבֹא שַׁוְעָתֵנוּ מִבֹּקֶר,

v'yayrö-eh rinu-naynu ad örev.   וְיֵרָאֶה רִנּוּנֵנוּ עַד עָרֶב.

Ya-aleh kolaynu may-erev,   יַעֲלֶה קוֹלֵנוּ מֵעֶרֶב,

v'yövo tzid'kö-saynu mi-boker,   וְיָבֹא צִדְקָתֵנוּ מִבֹּקֶר,

v'yayrö-eh fid-yo-naynu ad örev.   וְיֵרָאֶה פִּדְיוֹנֵנוּ עַד עָרֶב.

Ya-aleh inu-yaynu may-erev,   יַעֲלֶה עִנּוּיֵנוּ מֵעֶרֶב,

v'yövo s'lichö-saynu mi-boker,   וְיָבֹא סְלִיחָתֵנוּ מִבֹּקֶר,

v'yayrö-eh na-akösaynu ad örev.   וְיֵרָאֶה נַאֲקָתֵנוּ עַד עָרֶב.

Ya-aleh m'nusaynu may-erev,   יַעֲלֶה מְנוּסֵנוּ מֵעֶרֶב,

v'yövo l'ma-ano mi-boker,   וְיָבֹא לְמַעֲנוּ מִבֹּקֶר,

v'yayrö-eh chipu-raynu ad örev.   וְיֵרָאֶה כִּפּוּרֵנוּ עַד עָרֶב.

*May our supplications ascend at eventide; our pleas come [before You] in the
morning; and our prayers be favorably accepted until evening. May our voice*

ascend at eventide; our righteousness come [before You] in the morning; and our [prayer for] redemption be favorably accepted until evening. May our affliction ascend at eventide; our pardon come forth in the morning; and our cry be favorably accepted until evening. May [the merit of] our trust ascend at eventide; come [before Him] for His sake, in the morning; and our [petition for] atonement be favorably accepted until evening.

120. Yibö-neh ha-mikdösh, ir tziyon
t'malay, v'shöm nöshir shir
chödösh uvir'nönöh na-aleh.

‫120 . יִבָּנֶה הַמִּקְדָּשׁ, עִיר צִיּוֹן‬
‫תְּמַלֵּא, וְשָׁם נָשִׁיר שִׁיר‬
‫חָדָשׁ וּבִרְנָנָה נַעֲלֶה.‬

The Temple will be rebuilt, the city of Zion will be replenished, and there we shall sing a new song, and with praise we will go up.

121. Yifrach b'yömöv tzadik v'rov
shölom ad b'li yöray-ach. V'yayrd
miyöm ad yöm uminöhör ad af'say
öretz. L'fönöv yich-r'u tzi-yim
v'o-y'vöv öför y'la-chaychu.

‫121 . יִפְרַח בְּיָמָיו צַדִּיק וְרֹב‬
‫שָׁלוֹם עַד בְּלִי יָרֵחַ. וְיֵרְדְּ‬
‫מִיָּם עַד יָם וּמִנָּהָר עַד אַפְסֵי‬
‫אָרֶץ. לְפָנָיו יִכְרְעוּ צִיִּים‬
‫וְאֹיְבָיו עָפָר יְלַחֵכוּ.‬

May the righteous man flourish in his days, and the abundance of peace, until the moon shall be needed no more. May he have dominion from sea to sea, from the river until the end of the earth; let the inhabitants of the wilderness kneel before him and his enemies lick the dust.

122. Yis-m'chu hashöma-yim v'sögayl
hö-öretz, yir-am ha-yöm um'lo-o.

‫122 . יִשְׂמְחוּ הַשָּׁמַיִם וְתָגֵל‬
‫הָאָרֶץ, יִרְעַם הַיָּם וּמְלֹאוֹ.‬

The heavens will rejoice, the earth will exult; the sea and its fullness will roar.

123. Yis-m'chu v'mal'chus'chö
shom'ray shabös v'kor'ay oneg,
am m'kad'shay sh'vi-i, kulöm yis-b'u
v'yis-an'gu mituvechö, uvash'vi-i rötzisö
bo v'kidashto, chemdas yömim oso
körösö, zaycher l'ma-asay v'rayshis.

123. יִשְׂמְחוּ בְמַלְכוּתְךָ
שׁוֹמְרֵי שַׁבָּת וְקוֹרְאֵי עֹנֶג,
עַם מְקַדְּשֵׁי שְׁבִיעִי, כֻּלָּם יִשְׂבְּעוּ
וְיִתְעַנְּגוּ מִטּוּבֶךָ, וּבַשְּׁבִיעִי רָצִיתָ
בּוֹ וְקִדַּשְׁתּוֹ, חֶמְדַּת יָמִים אוֹתוֹ
קָרָאתָ, זֵכֶר לְמַעֲשֵׂה בְרֵאשִׁית.

Those who observe the Shabbat and call it a delight shall rejoice in Your kingship; the nation which hallows the Seventh Day – all shall be satiated and delighted with Your goodness. You were pleased with the Seventh Day and made it holy; You called it the most desirable of days, in remembrance of the work of Creation.

124. Yisrö-ayl b'tach ba-shem,
ezröm umöginöm hu.

124. יִשְׂרָאֵל בְּטַח בַּה׳,
עֶזְרָם וּמָגִנָּם הוּא.

Israel, trust in the Lord; He is their help and protector.

125. Y'min hashem romaymöh,
y'min hashem osöh chö-yil.

125. יְמִין ה׳ רוֹמֵמָה,
יְמִין ה׳ עֹשָׂה חָיִל.

The right hand of the Lord is exalted; the right hand of the Lord performs deeds of valor.

126. Yom zeh l'yisrö-ayl oröh
v'simchöh, shabös m'nuchöh.

126. יוֹם זֶה לְיִשְׂרָאֵל אוֹרָה
וְשִׂמְחָה, שַׁבָּת מְנוּחָה.

Tzivisö pikudim b'ma-amad har

צִוִּיתָ פִּקּוּדִים בְּמַעֲמַד הַר

si-nai, shabös umo-adim lish-mor

סִינַי, שַׁבָּת וּמוֹעֲדִים לִשְׁמוֹר

b'chöl shönai, la-aroch l'fönai mas-ays

בְּכָל שָׁנַי, לַעֲרוֹךְ לְפָנַי מַשְׂאֵת

va-aruchöh, shabös m'nuchöh.

וַאֲרוּחָה, שַׁבָּת מְנוּחָה.

Yom zeh l'yisrö-ayl

יוֹם זֶה לְיִשְׂרָאֵל

Chemdas hal'vövos l'umöh sh'vuröh,

חֶמְדַּת הַלְּבָבוֹת לְאֻמָּה שְׁבוּרָה,

lin'föshos nich-övos n'shömöh

לִנְפָשׁוֹת נִכְאָבוֹת נְשָׁמָה

y'sayröh, l'nefesh m'tzayröh tösir

יְתֵרָה, לְנֶפֶשׁ מְצֵרָה תָּסִיר

anöchöh, shabös m'nuchöh.

אֲנָחָה, שַׁבָּת מְנוּחָה.

Yom zeh l'yisrö-ayl

יוֹם זֶה לְיִשְׂרָאֵל

Kidashtö bay-rachtö oso miköl

קִדַּשְׁתָּ בֵּרַכְתָּ אוֹתוֹ מִכָּל

yömim, b'shayshes kilisö m'leches

יָמִים, בְּשֵׁשֶׁת כִּלִּיתָ מְלֶאכֶת

olömim, bo mö-tz'u agumim

עוֹלָמִים, בּוֹ מָצְאוּ עֲגוּמִים

hash-kayt uvit-chöh, shabös

הַשְׁקֵט וּבִטְחָה, שַׁבָּת

m'nuchöh. Yom zeh l'yisrö-ayl

מְנוּחָה. יוֹם זֶה לְיִשְׂרָאֵל

L'isur m'löchöh tzivisönu norö,

לְאִסּוּר מְלָאכָה צִוִּיתָנוּ נוֹרָא,

ez-keh hod m'luchöh im shabös

אֶזְכֶּה הוֹד מְלוּכָה אִם שַׁבָּת

esh-moröh, akriv shai lamorö,

אֶשְׁמֹרָה, אַקְרִיב שַׁי לַמּוֹרָא,

min-chöh merköchöh, shabös

מִנְחָה מֶרְקָחָה, שַׁבָּת

m'nuchöh. Yom zeh l'yisrö-ayl

מְנוּחָה. יוֹם זֶה לְיִשְׂרָאֵל

Chadaysh mikdöshaynu zöch'röh

חַדֵּשׁ מִקְדָּשֵׁנוּ זָכְרָה

139

ne-chere-ves, tuv'chö, moshi-aynu, נֶחֱרֶבֶת, טוּבְךָ, מוֹשִׁיעֵנוּ,

t'nöh la-ne-etzeves, b'shabös תְּנָה לַנֶּעֱצֶבֶת, בְּשַׁבָּת

yosheves b'zemer ush'vöchöh, יוֹשֶׁבֶת בְּזֶמֶר וּשְׁבָחָה,

shabös m'nuchöh. **Yom zeh l'yisrö-ayl** שַׁבָּת מְנוּחָה. יוֹם זֶה לְיִשְׂרָאֵל

This is Israel's special day, a day of light, of happiness and of rest, as You commanded us on Mount Sinai. It refreshes us with the gift of an extra soul. You made the world in six days and commanded us not to work on the seventh day. We know we will be rewarded if we keep Shabbat, but please, God, do not forget that the Temple is still to be rebuilt.

127. Yom zeh m'chuböd miköl yömim, ki vo shövas tzur olömim. **127.** יוֹם זֶה מְכֻבָּד מִכָּל יָמִים, כִּי בוֹ שָׁבַת צוּר עוֹלָמִים.

Shayshes yömim ta-aseh m'lachtechö, v'yom hash'vi-i laylo-kechö, shabös lo sa-aseh vo m'löchöh, ki chol ösöh shayshes yömim. **Yom zeh m'chuböd** שֵׁשֶׁת יָמִים תַּעֲשֶׂה מְלַאכְתֶּךָ, וְיוֹם הַשְּׁבִיעִי לֵאלֹקֶיךָ, שַׁבָּת לֹא תַעֲשֶׂה בוֹ מְלָאכָה, כִּי כָל עָשָׂה שֵׁשֶׁת יָמִים. יוֹם זֶה מְכֻבָּד

Rishon hu l'mikrö-ay kodesh, yom shaböson yom shabas kodesh, al kayn köl ish b'yayno y'kadaysh, al shtay lechem yiv-tz'u s'mimim. **Yom zeh m'chuböd** רִאשׁוֹן הוּא לְמִקְרָאֵי קֹדֶשׁ, יוֹם שַׁבָּתוֹן יוֹם שַׁבַּת קֹדֶשׁ, עַל כֵּן כָּל אִישׁ בְּיֵינוֹ יְקַדֵּשׁ, עַל שְׁתֵּי לֶחֶם יִבְצְעוּ תְמִימִם. יוֹם זֶה מְכֻבָּד

140

Echol mash-manim sh'say
mamtakim, ki kayl yitayn l'chol bo
d'vaykim, beged lilbosh lechem
chukim, bösör v'dögim v'chöl
mat-amim. **Yom zeh m'chuböd**

אֱכֹל מַשְׁמַנִּים שְׁתֵה
מַמְתַּקִּים, כִּי קֵל יִתֵּן לְכֹל בּוֹ
דְּבֵקִים, בֶּגֶד לִלְבּוֹשׁ לֶחֶם
חֻקִּים, בָּשָׂר וְדָגִים וְכָל
מַטְעַמִּים. יוֹם זֶה מְכֻבָּד

Lo sech-sar kol bo v'öchaltö,
v'sövö-tö uvay-rachtö, es
hashem elokechö asher öhavtö,
ki vay-rach'chö miköl hö-amim.
Yom zeh m'chuböd

לֹא תֶחְסַר כֹּל בּוֹ וְאָכַלְתָּ,
וְשָׂבָעְתָּ וּבֵרַכְתָּ, אֶת
ה' אֱלֹקֶיךָ אֲשֶׁר אָהַבְתָּ,
כִּי בֵרַכְךָ מִכָּל הָעַמִּים.
יוֹם זֶה מְכֻבָּד

Ha-shöma-yim m'sap'rim k'vodo,
v'gam hö-öretz mö-l'öh chasdo,
r'u ki chöl ay-leh ös'söh yödo,
ki hu ha-tzur pö-olo sömim.
Yom zeh m'chuböd

הַשָּׁמַיִם מְסַפְּרִים כְּבוֹדוֹ,
וְגַם הָאָרֶץ מָלְאָה חַסְדּוֹ,
רְאוּ כִּי כָל אֵלֶּה עָשְׂתָה יָדוֹ,
כִּי הוּא הַצּוּר פָּעֳלוֹ תָמִים.
יוֹם זֶה מְכֻבָּד

This is the most precious of days, because it is the day on which God rested. You should work for six days, but honor the seventh day as Shabbat. Make Kiddush, eat Challah and other good things. When you are sated, bless God as He has blessed you. The whole universe attests to God's glory and perfection.

128. Yösis öla-yich elo-kö-yich, kim'sos chösön al kalöh.

128. יָשִׂישׂ עָלַיִךְ אֱלֹקָיִךְ, כִּמְשׂוֹשׂ חָתָן עַל כַּלָּה.

Your God will rejoice over you as a bridegroom rejoices over his bride.

129. Y'vörech'chö hashem mitziyon, ur'ay b'tuv y'rushölö-yim kol y'may cha-yechö. Ur'ay vönim l'vönechö, shölom al yisrö-ayl.

129. יְבָרֶכְךָ ה' מִצִּיּוֹן, וּרְאֵה בְּטוּב יְרוּשָׁלָיִם כֹּל יְמֵי חַיֶּיךָ. וּרְאֵה בָנִים לְבָנֶיךָ, שָׁלוֹם עַל יִשְׂרָאֵל.

May the Lord bless you from Zion and may you see the prosperity of Jerusalem all the days of your life. May you live to see your children's children. May Israel have peace.

Selected English Songs

130. BIG GEDALIA GOOMBER

I'm big Gedalia Goomber,
I'm not exactly small,
I'm really not so very big,
just seventeen feet tall.

I'm rigged for heavy working,
for that I'm very fit,
six days a week I'm at it,
and on the seventh day I quit.

Chorus: Ain't gonna work on
Saturday, ain't gonna work on
Saturday, single, double, triple pay,
won't make me work on Saturday,
ain't gonna work on Saturday —
why? It's Shabbos *Kodesh*.

I once helped raise a building,
and on the hundredth floor,
I was carrying a load of bricks,
an easy ton or more. And here it's
late on Friday, I knew I had to stop,
so I yelled "Watch out below!" and
I let the whole thing drop. **Chorus.**

At driving a locomotive, I thought
I'd take a crack, I had the throttle
wide open, zooming down the track.
And here it's almost Shabbos,
the sun's about to set,
so I dived into a mud hole,
and the train is running yet.
Chorus.

I worked down in a coal mine,
and lost myself all right,

I couldn't tell the days apart,
because there was no light.
So I set myself to digging,
just as fast as you may please,
and popped up in an hour,
where the people speak Chinese.
Chorus.

I turned to deep sea diving,
and took an awful chance,
on a sunken steamer's deck,
I got caught by my pants.
And trapped beneath the ocean,
I couldn't set me free,
but I went home for Shabbos,
and I dragged that ship with me.
Chorus.

I once was an explorer,
to Africa I went, one Shabbos hungry
lions came roaring 'round my tent.
My assistant held my rifle,
"Go, Goomber, shoot those pests,"
but I invited them instead,
to be my Shabbos guests. **Chorus.**

143

worked at Cape Kennedy,
and things were running right,
A great big rocket ship was set,
on the launching site.
And here it's getting dark,
Shabbos was coming soon,
so I pushed the starting button,
And spent Shabbos on the moon.
Chorus.

once was an astronaut,
and flying through the stars,
came across a spaceship,
whose pilots were from Mars.
said, "Hello there, Martians!"
and stayed with them until,
taught them to keep Shabbos,
and they said, "We will, we will."
Chorus.

dress my best on Shabbos,
three meals I feast me fine,
make a royal Kiddush,
in a barrel full of wine.

And when I sing my Z'miros,
for a thousand miles they know,
that I'm enjoying Shabbos,
for Hashem has told us so.
Chorus.

131. JUST ONE SHABBOS

The Western Wall on Friday night,
his first time ever there,
strapped into his knapsack with
his long and curly hair,
he stood there for a while,
then broke out with a smile,
emotions overwhelming
joy with tears.

The men were dancing there,
their hearts so full of love,
they sang such happy tunes
to thank the One above,
for showing them the way,
for giving them a day, to rest,
rejoice, with peace of mind to pray.

Chorus:
Just one Shabbos and we'll all be free,
just one Shabbos come and join with me.
Let's sing and dance to the sky,
with our spirits so high,
we will show them all it's true,
let them come and join us too.

I said, hello my friend, you seem
to be amused, he said, much more
than that, I am a bit confused,
I know that I'm a Jew,
I was Bar Mitzva'd too,
but Shabbos in our home
whoever knew.

He asked to join with us,
to understand and see,
he spent some time with us in total
ecstasy, next Shabbos came along,
his feeling grew so strong,
he first began to feel
that he belonged.
Chorus.

He found this treasure made
some changes in his life,
a brand new family,
his children and his wife.
They learn new things each day,
to live the Torah way,
the message of the
Shabbos they'll relay.

Now every Friday night
they go down to the wall,
invite some people home
and they will tell them all,
we'll teach you this new song,
so join and sing along,
and soon we'll all be free
it won't be long. **Chorus.**

132. MY MOTHER'S SHABBOS CANDLES

Among the smiles, among the tears, of my
childhood, sweet and bitter years. There's
a picture that my memories fondly frames,
and through it shines two tiny flames.

My mother's Shabbos candles,
that made our home so bright,
which faithfully she lighted,
with a prayer on Friday night.

And then around the table,
we gathered and we heard,
my father chant the Kiddush,
his heart in every word.

Our humble home became a
mansion in that mystic glow,
our hearts were filled with hopes
and dreams and thoughts of long ago.

And yet the tragic stories
of Israel's darkest nights,
will never dim the glory,
of my mother's Shabbos light.

133. SOMEDAY WE WILL ALL BE TOGETHER

There learned in a dark frigid cellar,
alone just a small group of men,
when in rushed a soldier
and led them all away,

the flame of Torah flickered
on that day.

So many tears, so much sorrow,
the pain has lasted thousands of
years, but soon we'll stop crying,
the cruelty will end, *Melech
Ha-moshiach* will descend.

Chorus: Someday we will
all be together, someday we'll
be sheltered and warmed.
Never will we have to express
any fear, our scars and our
wounds will disappear.
Avraham and Yitzchak will
be there to greet us, Yaakov and
his sons will stand by and smile,
Moshe Rabbeinu will greet us
once again, in Yerushalayim,
with the help of Hashem.

We learn every day, and
we *Daaven*, we ask Hashem
please bring those old times back.
I know that He's listening,

He always does what's true,
for I've received His promise,
and so have you. That Hashem
will lead us out of this exile,
it won't be too much longer I know.
And then together we will *Daaven*,
together we'll all sing,
and praise and thank
Hashem for everything.
Chorus.

134. THE LITTLE BIRD
The little bird is calling,
it wishes to return.
The little bird is wounded,
it cannot fly but yearn.
It's captured by the vultures,
crying bitterly, "Oh, to see my
nest again, Oh, to be redeemed."

The little bird of silver,
so delicate and rare,
still chirps amongst the vultures,
outshining all that's there.
How long, how long it suffers,

how long will it be.
When will come the eagle,
and set the little bird free.

The little bird is Yisroel,
the vultures are our foes,
the painful wound is *Golus* (exile),
which we all feel and know,
the nest is Yerushalayim,
where we yearn to be once more,
the eagle is Moshiach,
whom we are waiting for.

135. THE TIME IS NOW
Standing still,
at the edge of time,
there waits a nation
for that final sign,
filled with dreams
of a land they know,
the home that they
were promised long ago.
Listen close and you'll
hear their song,
it tells of how they've waited

for so long. Yet they know
that the day is near, there is
something in the air that says...

Chorus: The time is now,
so keep on trying, here and now,
there's no denying, what we could
achieve if we would only believe,
one more mitzvah is all that we need.
Can't you tell, it's almost over, any
day, we'll hear that *Shofar* and then
when we do we'll know that *Golus*
(exile) is through, we can do it,
now is the time!

Time goes by and the
days are long, but we the
nation keep a faith that's strong.
Deep inside it's because we know,
that very soon it will be time to go.

Time to see why the world began,
to know the end of that eternal plan,
all along this was meant to be,
this is our destiny. And... **Chorus.**

Sound the call, it's almost over,
one and all, will hear that Shofar,
and then when we do we'll know
that Golus is through, we can do it,
listen well – The time is now!

136. TO LOVE A FELLOW JEW

To love a fellow Jew,
just the same as you,
is the basis of our holy Torah.
He may be far from me,
across the widest sea,
still I always love him
just the same.

For seventy, eighty years,
a soul may wear and tear,
just to do a favor for another.
Love him with all your heart,
the heavens spread apart,
and have your prayers
answered speedily.

148

137. WE'VE EXISTED SO LONG

We've existed so long,
for the Torah kept us strong,
and the Torah will never disappear.

Through the ages it was brought,
by our children who were taught,
to follow it and constantly declare:
I'm a Jew and I'm proud,
and I'll sing it aloud,
because forever that's what I'll be.
I'm a Jew and I'm proud,
and that's without a doubt,
because Hashem is always
watching over me.

138. WHO KNOWS ONE?

Who knows One? I know one!
One is Hashem, one is Hashem,
one is Hashem – in the heavens
and the earth.

Who knows Two? I know Two!
Two are the tablets which Moshe
brought. One is Hashem...

Who knows three? I know Three!
Three are the fathers. Two...

Who knows Four? I know Four!
Four are the mothers. Three...

Who knows Five? I know Five!
Five are the books of the Torah.
Four.....

Who knows Six? I know Six!
Six are the orders of the Mishnah.
Five...

Who knows Seven? I know Seven!
Seven are the days of the week. Six...

Who knows Eight? I know Eight!
Eight are the days 'til the Brit Milah.
Seven...

Who knows Nine? I know Nine!
Nine are the months 'til the baby's
born. Eight...

Who knows Ten? I know Ten!
Ten are the Ten Commandments.
Nine...

Who knows Eleven? I know Eleven!
Eleven are the stars of Yosaif's dream.
Ten..

Who knows Twelve? I know Twelve!
Twelve are the tribes of Israel.
Eleven...

Who knows Thirteen?
I know Thirteen! Thirteen are
the years 'till Bar mitzvah.
Twelve...

139. YOUNG FOLKS, OLD FOLKS

Chorus: Young folks, old folks,
everybody come, come to our
Jewish home and have a lot of fun.
Kiss the Mezuzah hanging on the
door, and you'll learn about the
Torah, like you've never
learned before.

Adam was the first man,
and Eve was his spouse,
in the Garden of Eden,
they started keeping house.
Everything was dandy,
and merry, on the main,
'till along came Abel,
and started raising Cain.
Chorus.

Noah was a carpenter,
who stumbled in the dark,
came across a hammer,
and built himself an ark.
Along came the animals,
two by two,
and then it started pouring,
as the skies were turning blue.
Chorus.

Avraham, the first Jew,
was a brave and daring kid,
believed in only one God,
when no one else did.
He smashed all the idols,
in his father's shop,
and when Terach came home,
he really blew his top.
Chorus.

When King Nimrod heard of this,
he flew into a rage, and sent his
heavy henchmen, to put Abe in
a cage. They threw him in the
furnace, to roast him to a coal,
but little Abe just stood there,
waving smartly to them all. **Chorus.**

Eisav was a hunter,
Yaakov was his brother,
one had a little, more than the other.
For his birthright, Eisav didn't really
care, so he sold it to Yaakov,
for a nickel and a beer. **Chorus.**

Yaakov had twelve sons,
each one became a tribe,
when someone grabbed Dinah,
they left no one alive.
One went into business,
one learned in his father's tent,
While Yaakov paid a fortune,
for the groceries and the rent. **Chorus.**

Yosef was the apple,

of his father's eye,
but his brothers dumped him,
and told a little lie.
Now his father Yaakov,
was left without a hunch,
thinking that his favorite son,
was eaten up for lunch. **Chorus.**

Moshe took the Jews,
from Pharaoh's wicked land,
he led them through the desert,
to the Promised Land.
When he struck the rock,
there rose a mighty cheer,
instead of water flowed,
Schlitz malt liquor beer. **Chorus.**

David was a shepherd,
who saved the Jewish race,
Goliath tumbled over,
when he looked at David's face.
Many were the victories,
when David was the king,
the enemy would drop dead,
when he began to sing. **Chorus.**

Daniel was a prisoner,
brought before the king,
they played twenty questions,
but couldn't learn a thing.
They threw him in a lion's den,
to perform a great feat,
so Daniel became a dentist,
and pulled the lion's teeth.
Chorus.

140. MY ZAIDY

My Zaidy lived with us
in my parents' home,
he used to laugh and put
me on his knee.

He spoke about his life in Poland,
he spoke with a bitter memory.
He spoke about the soldiers
who had beat him,
they laughed at him they
tore his long black coat.
He spoke about a synagogue
that they burned down,

and the crying that was
heard beneath the smoke.

Chorus:
But Zaidy made us laugh,
and Zaidy made us sing,
and Zaidy made a Kiddush
Friday night. And Zaidy,
Oh my Zaidy how I loved him so,
and Zaidy used to teach me
wrong from right.

His eyes lit up when he would
teach me Torah, he taught me
every line so carefully.
He spoke about our slavery
in Egypt, and how God took
us out to make us free. **Chorus.**

Winter went by, and summer
came along, I went to camp to
run and play. And when I came
back home they said: Zaidy's gone,
and all his books were packed
and stored away. **Chorus.**

I don't how or why it came to be,
it happened slowly over many years.
We just stopped being Jewish like
my Zaidy was, and no one cared
enough to shed a tear. **Chorus.**

Many winters went by,
many summers came along,

and now my children
sit in front of me.

And who will be the Zaidy of my
children, who will be their Zaidy if
not me? Who will be the Zaidys of our
children? Who will be their Zaidys if
not we? **Chorus.**

Questions & Answers

Candle Lighting

Q: What is the significance of the Shabbat and Festival candle lighting?

A: These are days of spiritual light, and we introduce them by kindling material light in this world.

Q: It is past 18 minutes to sunset on Friday afternoon, what should I do?

A: If it is still before sunset, you should light the candles, but if it is past sunset, you should not light the candles. (Check your local Jewish calendar for the proper candle lighting times.)

Q: Why are the hands drawn around the candles and toward the face?

A: This symbolizes our beckoning in of the Shabbat, bringing to our eyes and introducing into our heart the lights of the Shabbos candles.

Q: Can men light the Shabbat candles?

A: If there are no women in the household who are lighting the candles, then men should light the candles (following the same procedure).

The *Kiddush*

Q: What is the significance of *Sholom Alaychem* and the *Aishes Chayil* that follows?

A: In *Sholom Alaychem,* we greet the heavenly angels who accompany us home from the synagogue on Friday evening. In *Aishes Chayil,* we praise the wife of excellence.

Q: Why is the Kiddush recited over wine or grape juice?

A: These are traditional sacramental beverages.

Q: What if wine or grape juice are not available, or cannot be used for medical reasons?

A: Then the Kiddush is recited over Challah.

Q: Can a woman recite the Kiddush?

A: The obligation of Kiddush is given equally to men and to women; however, just as it is customary for a woman to recite the blessing over the candles, it is customary for men to recite the Kiddush. If there are no men present to recite the Kiddush, then women should recite the Kiddush following the same procedure.

Q: Why do we stand during the Kiddush?

A: It is an act of honor to the mitzvah, to stand and show one's deference.

Q: Why are the Challot covered during the Kiddush?

A: This symbolizes the layer of protective dew which covered the manna, given to the Jews in the desert on each Friday for Shabbat.

The Meal

Q: What is the significance of the two loaves of Challah?

A: It represents the double portion of manna given to the Jews in the desert on each Friday for Shabbat.

Q: My hands are clean, why do I need to wash them prior to eating Challah or bread?

A: The washing of the hands is a continuation of the ritual washing that the priests performed in the Temple, before partaking of the sacrificial food and *T'rumah*.

Q: Why don't we talk between the washing of the hands and the partaking of the Challah?

A: So that we do not make an interruption between the blessing and the performance of the mitzvah.

Questions & Answers

Q: Why do we dip the piece of *Challah* (bread) in salt?

A: To remind us that our table should be as holy as the altar, upon which salt was offered with every sacrifice.

Grace After Meals

Q: What is the significance of the washing of the fingertips before the Grace After a Meal?

A: In honor of the blessing, we wash off any dirt that has accumulated during the meal.

The Havdalah

Q: What is the significance of the Havdalah?

A: Just as we make a distinction of entering the Shabbat by kindling the Shabbat candles, we make a distinction to mark the departure of Shabbat by performing the Havdalah.

Q: Why do we recite the blessing over sweet aromatic spices?

A: During Shabbat we are granted an extra potential for spirituality, which departs along with the Shabbat. We "revive" the soul with the fragrance of sweet aromatic spices.

Q: Why do we recite the blessing over fire?

A: Shabbat is a day of God's light. Kindling fire, on the other hand, is a human activity, symbolizing our efforts to create and generate life in the world during the coming week, which we have now entered.

Q: Why do we fold our fingers over our thumb and look at our fingernails following the blessing over fire?

A: Since a blessing must precede an action, we therefore make use of the light. This is accomplished by looking at our fingernails.

Song Number Index

Achas Sho-alti	1	Im Ōmar'ti	42
Adon Olōm	2	Ivdu Es Hashem B'simchōh	43
Ain Aroch L'chō	3	Just One Shabbos	131
Al Hanisim	4	K'ayōl Ta-arog	44
Al Ha-sela	5	Kayl Hahodō-os	45
Al Tirō	6	Kayl N'kōmos Hashem	46
Am Yisrō-ayl Chai	7	Kayli Atōh	47
Ani Ma-amin	8	Kaytzad M'rakdim	48
Ani Ōmarti	9	Ki Elokim Yoshi-a Tziyon	49
An-im Z'miros	10	Ki Haym Cha-yaynu	50
Asadayr Li-s'udōsō	11	Ki L'chō Tov	51
Asher Bōrō	12	Ki Lo Yitosh	52
Ashraynu	13	Ki Mitziyon	53
Atōh Hōkayl	14	Ki V'simchōh	54
Atōh V'chartōnu	15	Ko Ōmar	55
Ayleh Chōmdōh	16	Kō Ribon Ōlam	56
Aylechō Hashem Ekrō	17	Kōl Hō-olōm Kulo	57
Ayleh Vōrechev	18	L'ma-an Achai	59
Ayli-yōhu Hanōvi	19	Latyv Tōhor	58
Aytz Cha-yim	20	Lo Yisō Goy	60
Azamayr Bish'vōchin	21	L'shōnōh Habō-ōh	61
B'cō Bōtchu	22	Lulay He-emanti	62
B'chō Hashem	23	Mipi Kayl	64
Big Gedalia Goomber	130	Mal'chus'chō	65
Bōruch Hagever	24	Mi Hu Zeh V'ayzeh Hu	66
Bōruch Hu	25	Mikolos Ma-yim Rabim	67
Bōruch Kayl Elyon	26	Mimitzra-yim G'altōnu	68
D'ror Yikra	27	Min Ha-maytzar	69
Da-yaynu	28	M'kimi May-ōfōr Dōl	70
Dōvid Melech Yisrō-ayl	29	M'nuchōh V'simchōh	71
Essō Aynay	30	Modeh Ani L'fōnechō	72
Hal'lu Es Hashem	32	My Mother's Shabbos Candles	132
Harninu Laylokim	31	My Zaidy	140
Hashem Z'chōrōnu	34	Nōchon Libi	73
Ha-Tov Ki Lo Chōlu	35	Nodōh Bi-hudōh	74
Ha-Ven Yakir Li	31	N'ye Zhuritzi Chlōptzi	75
Hinay Mah Tov Umah Nō-im	36	Od Yishōma	76
Hōrachamōn Hu Yanchi-laynu	37	Or Zōru-a	77
Hōrachamōn Hu Yishlach Lōnu	38	Oseh Shōlom	78
Hoshi-ōh Es Amechō	39	Ōshirōh La-shem	79
Hu Elokaynu	40	Ōvinu Malkaynu	80
Ilu Hotzi-ōnu	28	Ōvinu Malkaynu II	81
Im Atem	41	Ōvinu Ōv Hōrachamōn	82

Song Number Index

Ŏvo Big-vuros............................ 83	V'elokim Malki Mi-kedem........................... 110
Pis-chu Li.................................. 84	V'har'kosi Lŏchem B'rŏchŏh........................106
Rachamŏnŏ D'ŏnay........................ 85	V'hi She-ŏmdŏh.......................................111
Rachaym B'chasd'chŏ................... 86	V'hŏ-ayr Aynaynu.....................................107
Rom'mu Hashem......................... 87	V'hŏ-yŏh Ba-Yom Hahu............................108
Samach T'samach........................ 88	V'hŏ-yu Lim'shisŏh..................................112
She-yibŏneh Bays Hamikdŏsh.................... 89	V'kŏrayv P'zuraynu.................................113
Sh'ma Yisrŏ-ayl........................... 90	V'li-rushŏla-yim......................................114
Sh'sulim.................................. 91	V'nikaysi Dŏmŏm......................................115
Sim Shŏlom Tovŏh Uv'rŏchŏh...................... 92	V'sŏmachtŏ B'chagechŏ...........................116
Simŏn Tov................................. 93	V'ya-azor V'yŏgayn................................. 117
Someday We Will All Be Together.............133	We've Existed So Long............................. 137
S'u Sh'ŏrim Rŏshaychem........................... 94	Who Knows One?................................... 138
T'ra-naynŏh S'fŏsai....................... 95	Y'did Nefesh...118
The Little Bird..........................134	Ya-aleh Tachanu-naynu...........................119
The Time Is Now.........................135	Yibŏneh Hamikdŏsh................................ 120
To Love a Fellow Jew........................136	Yifrach..121
Torah Tzivŏh Lnu......................... 96	Yis-m'chu Hashŏma-yim............................. 122
Tzavay Y'shuŏs Yaakov........................ 97	Yis-m'chu V'mal'chus'chŏ.........................123
Tziyon Halo Tish-ali..................... 98	Yisrŏ-ayl B'tach Ba-hashem.......................124
Tzŏm-ŏh L'chŏ Nafshi................... 99	Y'min Hashem......................................125
Tzur Mishelo...........................100	Yom Zeh L'yisrŏ-ayl...............................126
U-fŏratz-tŏ.............................101	Yom Zeh M'chubŏd.................................. 127
Ush'avtem Ma-yim......................102	Yosis Ŏla-yich...................................... 128
Uv'chayn Tzadikim.....................103	Young Folks, Old Folks............................ 139
V'chŏl Karnay..........................109	Y'vŏrech'chŏ...129
V'chŏl Ma-aminim......................105	

לזכות

הרב הת׳ יוסף בן חי׳ מלכה שיחי׳
מרת חנה פריווא בת אלטער יהושע הכהן ע״ה

הרב הת׳ שניאור זלמן בן חנה פריווא
מרת דבורה גבריאלה בת רייזא פייגא
חנה פריווא בת דבורה גבריאלה
הינדא גאלדא בת דבורה גבריאלה
דוד משה יהודה בן דבורה גבריאלה
מנחם מענדל בן מרים שרה
מניא שיינא בת מרים שרה
שיחיו לאורך ימים ושנים טובות

MORE POPULAR CHOICES FROM OUR "COMPANION SERIES"

The Shabbat Synagogue Companion: Explains Prayers for Shabbat Eve and Shabbat Day
A complete guide to both Friday evening and Shabbat morning prayer services, the Companion maps every prayer and explains its origin and meaning. It includes English transliterations of many key prayers and instructions for performing common synagogue honors such as opening the Ark and being called to the Torah. *Softcover; 6.5x5.5; 160 pages; JLG-02; ISBN 1-891293-12-5.*

The Kabbalat Shabbat Synagogue Companion: Transliterations and Explanations
Presenting the complete Friday evening service, along with easy-to-read English transliterations, clear instructions, and a concise overview of Shabbat and prayer. This plain language guide will enable you to pray, sing, and comprehend the services at a higher level. *Softcover; 6.5x5.5; 160 pages; JLG-04; ISBN 1-891293-14-1. (Audio available)*

The Complete Junior Congregation Synagogue Companion: For Children in the Synagogue
Designed for beginners of all ages, this companion brings the Shabbat synagogue experience to life. It features the basic Shabbat prayers in clear Hebrew type, alongside easy-to-read English transliterations, and easy to understand English translations and explanations so everyone will be able to join in and enjoy the prayer services like never before. *Softcover; 6.5x5.5; 160 pages; JLG-08; ISBN 1-891293-19-2.*

The High Holiday Synagogue Companion: Transliterations and Explanations
Your personal guide to and through the Rosh Hashanah and Yom Kippur prayerbook. It explains what prayers are found on each page, their origin, meaning, and the proper action required at each point, and includes key prayers as well as many inspirational readings and stories. *Softcover; JLG-03; ISBN 1-891293-10-9.*

The Passover Seder Table Companion: Transliterated Hagaddah and Explanations
The entire Hagaddah transliterated! Guides you step-by-step through the Passover Seder and all its preparations. Includes a clear and concise overview of Passover, easy-to-read English transliterations, clear instruction, plus a collection of over 50 popular holiday songs. *Softcover; 6.5x5.5; 160 pages; JLG-06; ISBN 1-891293-17-6.*

The Complete Jewish Wedding Companion: Guide to a Traditional Jewish Wedding
The ultimate guide to understanding and enjoying a traditional Jewish wedding experience. Contains clear instructions, explanations, and directions, plus all relevant prayers, liturgy, and blessings. *Softcover; 6.5x5.5; 128 pages; JLG-07; ISBN 1-891293-18-4*